Fertilizer Use in African Agriculture

Fertilizer Use in African Agriculture

Lessons Learned and Good Practice Guidelines

Michael Morris
Valerie A. Kelly
Ron J. Kopicki
Derek Byerlee

THE WORLD BANK
Washington, DC

1818 H Street, NW
Washington, DC 20433
Telephone: 202-473-1000
Internet: www.worldbank.org
E-mail: feedback@worldbank.org

1 2 3 4 :: 10 09 08 07

ISBN-10: 0-8213-6880-X
ISBN-13: 978-0-8213-6880-0
e-ISBN: 0-8213-6881-8
DOI: 10.1596/978-0-8213-6880-0

Cover photo: Aleksander Kawalec, FAO.

Library of Congress Cataloging-in-Publication Data has been applied for.

Contents

Boxes

Figures

Tables

Preface and Acknowledgments

This report and the companion *Africa Fertilizer Policy Toolkit* are intended to support better decision making by those interested in promoting fertilizer use as a way of stimulating economically efficient, environmentally friendly, pro-poor growth in agriculture. The discussion topics, examples, box features, and good practice guidelines have been selected for their relevance to Sub-Saharan Africa. Readers working in other developing regions may also find the materials useful.

The analysis and recommendations that follow are grounded in the belief that viable fertilizer markets, led by the private sector, must develop to increase and sustain fertilizer use over the longer term. The demand and supply of fertilizer exhibit several characteristics that reduce the profitability of buying and selling fertilizer and complicate the development of fertilizer markets, especially during the early stages of agricultural transformation. Examples of the challenges that often must be overcome to avoid market failure include strong seasonality in demand for fertilizer, the riskiness of using fertilizer (stemming from weather-related production variability and uncertain crop prices), highly dispersed demand for fertilizer, lack of purchasing power on the part of many potential users of fertilizer, the bulkiness of most fertilizer products, and the need to achieve large volumes of throughput in fertilizer procurement and distribution to capture economies of scale. Overcoming these challenges requires coordinated interventions in a number of areas.

This report does not present a detailed theoretical analysis of fertilizer supply-and-demand issues, nor does it provide guidance on the amounts of fertilizer that farmers in specific locations should apply to particular crops. Rather, it sketches out a conceptual framework to guide thinking about fertilizer policy and market development. The conceptual framework is intended to be practical, empirical, and above all useful. In addition, the report describes innovative strategic interventions to improve fertilizer market performance, and it summarizes lessons from past and current efforts to increase the efficiency and sustainability of fertilizer use.

Additional readings are cited that may be of interest. In this context, it is worth mentioning three discussion papers about fertilizer that were prepared as background pieces: Crawford, Jayne, and Kelly (2006); Kelly (2006); Gregory and Bumb (2006). Noteworthy as well is a fourth discussion paper summarizing the conclusions of an e-forum that was organized to tap into the wealth of practical knowledge that exists among practitioners about the challenges and opportunities faced by those working with fertilizer in Africa: Poulton, Dorward, and Kydd (2006).

The primary audiences for this report include government policy analysts and decision makers who are responsible for designing and implementing policies to promote efficient and sustainable use of fertilizer, as well as partners in the development community who are engaged in the policy dialogue. Secondary audiences for this report—but the primary audiences for the toolkit—include government officials, development agency representatives, and employees of development organizations, including nongovernmental organizations, involved in the design and implementation of projects to promote efficient and sustainable use of fertilizer. In addition, the report may be of interest to representatives from the agribusiness sector engaged in producing, importing, or distributing fertilizer.

This report was prepared by a team of staff and consultants from the Africa Region of the World Bank. It is one of several outputs of the Africa Fertilizer Strategy Assessment, an Analytical and Advisory Activity carried out with financial support from the U.K. Department for International Development. The World Bank team included Michael Morris (Team Leader), Valerie A. Kelly, Ron J. Kopicki, Derek Byerlee, Jeanette Sutherland, Yesmeana Butler, and Karen Brooks. Research assistance was provided by James Keough. Important contributions were also made by the authors of three specially commissioned background papers:

Eric Crawford, Thom Jayne, and Valerie A. Kelly of Michigan State University and Ian Gregory and Balu Bumb of the International Fertilizer Development Center. Colin Poulton, Andrew Dorward, and Jonathan Kydd of Imperial College London moderated an e-forum about fertilizer use in Africa and summarized key findings and recommendations in a moderators' synthesis paper that provided additional input into this report. Madhur Gautam, Robert Townsend, and Matthew MacMahon of the World Bank served as peer reviewers. John English and Jock Anderson reviewed early drafts and contributed many useful comments and suggestions. Joseph Baah-Dwomoh, John McIntire, Sushma Ganguly, and Kevin Cleaver of the World Bank supported the study and ensured that resources were available for its implementation. Valerie Kelly's contribution to the development of the Africa Fertilizer Policy Toolkit CD was funded in part by the Food Security III Cooperative Agreement between Michigan State University and the United States Agency for International Development.

A special debt of gratitude is owed to the authors of 17 case studies that reviewed previous efforts to promote increased fertilizer use in Africa and identified lessons learned: Akin Adesina, John Allgood (coauthor), Jo Anderson, Jim Bingen, Malcolm Blackie, Virginie Briand, Chris Dowswell, Liz Drake, Ian Gregory, Rob Groot, Larry Hammond, Valerie A. Kelly, Ron J. Kopicki, David Rohrbach, Paul Seward (coauthor), Jeanette Sutherland, David Tschirley, and Suhas Wani.

Acronyms and Abbreviations

ACF	Agricultural Consultative Forum
AGSF	Agricultural Management, Marketing, and Finance Service
CAADP	Comprehensive Africa Agriculture Development Programme
CIMMYT	Centro Internacional de Mejoramiento de Maíz y Trigo (International Maize and Wheat Improvement Center)
CV	coefficient of variation
DAP	diammonium phosphate
DFID	Department for International Development (U.K.)
FAI	Fertiliser Association of India
FAO	Food and Agriculture Organization
FIL	financial intermediary loan
FOB	free on board
FSP	Fertilizer Support Programme
FSRP	Food Security Research Project
GDP	gross domestic product
GIS	geographic information system

ha	hectare
IAAE	International Association of Agricultural Economists
IFDC	International Fertilizer Development Center
IFPRI	International Food Policy Research Institute
IIED	International Institute for Environment and Development
IITA	International Institute for Tropical Agriculture
K	potassium
kg	kilogram
KIT	Koninklijk Instituut voor de Tropen (Royal Tropical Institute, Amsterdam)
MACO	Ministry of Agriculture and Cooperatives (Zambia)
MT	metric ton
N	nitrogen or nutrient
NARS	national agricultural research system
NEPAD	New Partnership for Africa's Development
NGO	nongovernmental organization
ODI	Overseas Development Institute
P	phosphorus/price
PADEP	Participatory Agricultural Development and Empowerment Project
SADC	Southern Africa Development Community
SCODP	Sustainable Community-Oriented Development Programme
SSSA	Soil Science Society of America
SWC	soil and water conservation
TIP	Targeted Inputs Program
TSP	triple super phosphate
UN	United Nations
UNEP	United Nations Environment Programme
USAID	United States Agency for International Development
VCR	value-cost ratio
WARDA	West Africa Rice Development Association

CHAPTER 1

Introduction and Overview

The striking contrast between the limited use of fertilizer in Africa[1] and the much more extensive use of fertilizer in other developing regions has stimulated not only considerable discussion about the role of fertilizer in the agricultural development process but also debate about what types of policies and programs are needed to realize the potential benefits of fertilizer in African agriculture. This report summarizes key lessons learned from past efforts to promote fertilizer in Africa, provides an overview of the current state of knowledge concerning technical aspects of fertilizer use in Africa, and presents good practice guidelines for promoting sustainable increases in fertilizer use.

In every region of the world, the intensification of crop-based agriculture has been associated with a sharp increase in the use of chemical fertilizer. Given the generally low levels of fertilizer use in Africa, there can be little doubt that fertilizer use must increase in Africa if the region is to meet its agricultural growth targets, poverty reduction goals, and environmental sustainability objectives. For this reason, policies and programs are needed to encourage fertilizer use in ways that are technically efficient, economically rational, and market-friendly.

At the same time, it is important to recognize that fertilizer is not a panacea for all of the problems that afflict African agriculture and that promoting fertilizer in isolation from other needed actions will have little lasting impact. Many fertilizer promotion schemes implemented in Africa have succeeded in temporarily increasing use of fertilizer, but only in ways that have encouraged application of fertilizer at nonoptimal levels, imposed heavy administrative and fiscal burdens on governments, and undermined the development of viable commercial fertilizer markets. Relying on the same approaches used in the past is undesirable, because these approaches cannot be sustained over the longer term without continuous heavy infusions of financial support that few, if any, African countries can afford.

Fortunately, some interventions have worked reasonably well in paving the way for the emergence of technically efficient and economically sustainable private sector–led fertilizer markets. Several of the most promising of these interventions are discussed below. Practical guidance on selecting an appropriate package of interventions tailored to the needs of a particular country or of a region within a country is provided in the *Africa Fertilizer Policy Toolkit*, which is being produced as a companion to this report.

Low Fertilizer Use Is a Problem in Africa

Low fertilizer use is one of the factors explaining lagging agricultural productivity growth in Africa. In 2002, the most recent year for which data are available, the average intensity of fertilizer use in Sub-Saharan Africa was only 8 kilograms per hectare of cultivated land, much lower than in other developing regions. Even when countries and crops in similar agroecological zones are compared, the rate of fertilizer use is much lower in Africa than in other developing regions, and crop yields are correspondingly lower.

African soils present inherent difficulties for agriculture, and land-use practices during the past several decades have exacerbated those difficulties through nutrient mining by crops, leaching, and inadequate erosion control. Africa's land degradation problems can be attributed to many causes, but analysts generally agree that a fundamental contributing factor has been the failure by most farmers to intensify agricultural production in a manner that maintains soil fertility. The inherent lack of fertility, along with widespread soil nutrient mining, has led to expansion of the agricultural frontier in Africa and the opening up of less favorable soils for cultivation. This is a scenario for disaster over the long run, given the difficulty of restoring tropical soils to productive capacity. In many tropical soils, the restoration of organic matter—a key component in soil fertility—is a very long-term proposal, and in lateritic[2] soils such as those found throughout large parts of Africa, restoration may even be impossible. So without nutrient replenishment, many African farmers risk taking their soil resource base beyond a point of no return.

What can be done to address the problem? Organic fertilizers, where they are available, can and should be an integral component of soil fertility management strategies, but organic fertilizers alone will not be sufficient to support the sustained high productivity and production levels that will be necessary to feed Africa's rapidly growing population. There are simply not enough supplies of organic fertilizer, and the dwindling availability of uncultivated land limits the scope for increased fallowing. In this context, there is widespread agreement that needed improvements in soil fertility will require substantial increases in the use of inorganic fertilizers. An additional implication is that soil fertility should be a priority not only for African governments but also for the development community more generally, because it would be difficult to justify continuing to invest in an agriculture that is exhausting its own resource base.

Past Efforts to Promote Fertilizer in Africa

In considering future strategies for increasing fertilizer use in Africa, policy makers and the development agencies with whom they partner would be well advised to heed the lessons of the past. Efforts to promote fertilizer use in Africa have a long and varied history, and there is much to be learned from what has already been done.

During the 1970s and early 1980s, fertilizer programs in Africa were often characterized by large, direct government expenditures using various entry points to stimulate fertilizer demand and ensure supply. Interventions frequently included

- direct subsidies that reduced fertilizer prices paid by farmers,
- government-financed and -managed input credit programs,
- centralized control of fertilizer procurement and distribution activities, and
- centralized control of key output markets (with the goal of stabilizing prices and linking input and output markets to ensure smoother credit management).

Fertilizer promotion programs based on these types of interventions generally did not lead to sustained growth in fertilizer use. They often failed because

- the high fiscal and administrative costs were unsustainable;
- governments lacked capacity to implement them effectively; and
- designed with a "one-size-fits-all" philosophy, they failed to recognize the diversity of production systems and the range of farmers' needs.

During the 1980s and 1990s, fiscal deficits caused in part by agricultural support programs, along with donor pressure, brought about a change in course regarding fertilizer promotion strategies. The most salient changes included privatization or dissolution of government input supply agencies and liberalization of the fertilizer sector (for example, removal of price controls, elimination of subsidies, and dismantling of state fertilizer distribution agencies). Although these reforms had generally positive impacts on government budgets, they resulted in significant reductions in overall levels of fertilizer use and increased food insecurity among many rural households.

More recently, some policy makers have started to reconsider the prevailing thinking about promoting fertilizer. Noting that private firms have not always stepped in to fill the vacuum left by the withdrawal of state agencies from the fertilizer sector, they have called for the reengagement of the public sector in the importation and distribution of fertilizer. Concerned by the continuing low use of fertilizer by poor rural households, including many whose members suffer from chronic food insecurity, some have revived arguments that the role of the state should be expanded to include not only commercial marketing of fertilizer but also targeted distribution of subsidized fertilizer to poor households that lack the resources needed to purchase fertilizer on a commercial basis. The calls to reengage the public sector in fertilizer marketing and especially the arguments supporting the use of fertilizer subsidies to provide a safety net for the poor have sparked a lively policy debate that shows little sign of abating.

Factors Explaining Low Fertilizer Use in Africa

Many initiatives have been launched in Africa to remove fertilizer market distortions and harness the power of the private sector to procure fertilizer and deliver it to farmers, yet use of fertilizer continues to grow very slowly in most African countries. Why is this?

Evidence reviewed in this report suggests that the low use of fertilizer in Africa can be explained by demand-side as well as supply-side factors. Demand for fertilizer is often weak in Africa because incentives to use fertilizer are undermined by the low level and high variability of crop yields on the one hand and the high level of fertilizer prices relative to crop prices on the other. The demand-depressing effects of unfavorable price incentives are aggravated by many other factors, including the general lack of market information about the availability and cost of fertilizer, the inability of many farmers to raise the resources needed to purchase fertilizer, and the lack of knowledge on the part of many farmers about how to use fertilizer efficiently.

These constraints on the demand side are mirrored on the supply side by factors that reduce the timely availability of affordable fertilizer in the market. In many African countries, private investment in fertilizer distribution is discouraged by an unfavorable business climate characterized by excessive regulations, an abundance of taxes and fees, and high levels of rent seeking. As a result, fertilizer marketing is left mainly in the hands of inefficient public agencies. More fundamentally—and regardless of whether it is being done by public agencies or private firms—fertilizer distribution is unprofitable in many parts of Africa because of the weak and dispersed nature of demand, the small market size, high transportation costs stemming from inadequate road and rail infrastructure, and the limited availability and high cost of financing.

Need for an Integrated Approach to Promoting Fertilizer

Despite the many initiatives that have been launched to liberalize and privatize fertilizer markets in Africa, little progress has been made toward developing the type of enabling environment that is needed for a smooth and rapid transition from state-run to private sector–led marketing systems. So what can be done?

A key lesson that emerges from past efforts to promote increased fertilizer use in Africa is that there is a need for much clearer thinking about how fertilizer policy fits into a country's overall development strategy. In recent years, expectations have increased regarding the role that fertilizer can play in the economic development process. Once viewed mainly as a productivity-enhancing input for agriculture, today fertilizer is seen by many policy makers and even some development partners as a tool that can be used to achieve a range of broad development goals, including stimulating rapid economic growth, alleviating poverty, and protecting the rural poor in times of crisis. Some of these expectations are frankly unrealistic. Increased use of fertilizer can contribute to a range of objectives, including (in some cases) welfare objectives, but the size and the sustainability of the contribution that fertilizer can make will be limited, especially if underlying structural problems in the economy remain unaddressed.

Entry Points for Public Interventions

In considering possible entry points for public interventions to increase fertilizer use in Africa, it is important to adopt a long-term perspective. Efforts to promote fertilizer have all too often focused narrowly on stimulating immediate increases in fertilizer use with the help of fertilizer price subsidies—budgetary payments made by governments or development partners to reduce the cost of fertilizer at the farm level. This approach is very limited, however, because governments can do many things to promote fertilizer beyond artificially reducing the cost to farmers through direct price subsidies, and in fact other measures will often be more cost-effective and more financially sustainable. Public interventions can be used to help farmers, but they can also be used to help fertilizer importers and manufacturers, fertilizer distributors at the wholesale and retail levels, financial services providers, and other key actors on the supply side. More fundamentally, public interventions can involve not only direct budgetary payments designed to influence fertilizer prices in the short run, but also a wide range of other measures that improve the profitability of fertilizer over the medium to long run by directly or indirectly influencing market prices, costs incurred, or benefits received by consumers and producers of fertilizer.

If lasting solutions are to be found to redress Africa's fertilizer crisis, policy makers and development partners must work to identify and implement interventions aimed at addressing the underlying structural problems that undermine incentives for farmers to use fertilizer and for firms to supply fertilizer.

Public interventions that can be used to strengthen *demand for fertilizer* include

- strengthening agricultural research and extension (for example, by increasing support to organizations that conduct crop management research and by sponsoring on-farm fertilizer trials and demonstrations),
- improving farmers' ability to purchase fertilizer (for example, by improving their access to credit or by introducing cost-sharing mechanisms such as matching grants),

- providing farmers with financial tools to better manage risk (for example, by introducing innovative insurance instruments tailored to the needs of farmers—such as weather-indexed crop insurance),
- improving market information (for example, by increasing investment in market information systems and building capacity in the private sector to manage such systems on a commercial basis),
- protecting farmers against low and volatile output prices (for example, by investing in measures to reduce production variability—such as irrigation, research on drought-tolerant crops, and grain storage systems),
- empowering farmers by supporting producer organizations (for example, by increasing investment in rural education and by offering farmers training in organizational management skills), and
- improving the agricultural resource base so that use of fertilizer can be more profitable (for example, by investing in soil and water conservation measures and irrigation infrastructure).

Public interventions that can be used to strengthen *supply of fertilizer* include

- reducing fertilizer sourcing costs (for example, by lowering trade barriers, adopting common quality standards, and harmonizing approval processes to increase the size of national and regional markets, which would allow fertilizer importers and eventually manufacturers to capture economies of size and scope),
- reducing fertilizer distribution costs (for example, by improving road and rail infrastructure to reduce high transport costs),
- strengthening business finance and risk management instruments (for example, by implementing credit guarantee schemes and innovative types of insurance), and
- improving supply chain coordination mechanisms (for example, by enacting and enforcing regulations relating to product grades and standards and by introducing market information systems that can help to reduce information costs).

All of these measures, regardless of their focus, can potentially contribute to increased use of fertilizer in Africa. At the same time, none is likely to be effective if implemented in isolation. Policy makers and development partners who are seeking to bring about sustainable increases in fertilizer use must select combinations of these measures to ensure that demand and supply can grow in parallel, thereby providing the basis for the emergence of viable private sector–led commercial fertilizer markets.

What Role for Fertilizer Subsidies?

Where does this leave fertilizer subsidies? Fertilizer subsidies were tried in many African countries during the 1960s and 1970s, but after failing to live up to expectations, they were generally phased out as part of the liberalization and privatization reforms that started during the 1980s. More recently, there have been new calls to reintroduce fertilizer subsidies as a way of kick-starting fertilizer use, improving food security at the micro and macro levels, and stimulating the development of sustainable input markets. One leading proponent of fertilizer subsidies has been Jeffrey Sachs, who has advocated large-scale distribution of low-cost or no-cost fertilizer as a way of helping African smallholders escape the so-called poverty trap. Sachs's arguments have struck a chord with some African political leaders, as evidenced during the Africa Fertilizer Summit held in Abuja, Nigeria, in June 2006, where the case in favor of fertilizer subsidies was argued by a number of participants.

The political appeal of fertilizer subsidies is understandable. For politicians, fertilizer subsidies can be used to pursue important policy goals such as increasing agricultural productivity, improving food security, and reducing poverty and hunger. At the same time, fertilizer subsidies also provide a convenient instrument for channeling income support to large numbers of constituents, many of whom may be very poor and deserving of public assistance. Lamentably, however, measures that are politically popular are not always economically efficient or fiscally sustainable. Case study evidence from many African countries consistently shows that the cost of policies and programs designed to subsidize fertilizer prices has been very high, draining public coffers of scarce resources that could be spent more productively in other areas such as agricultural research, agricultural extension, farmer training, and so forth. More important, fertilizer price subsidies offer limited prospects for effecting lasting solutions to the problem of low fertilizer use, because simply making fertilizer cheaper for farmers does little to build the basis for sustainable market-led fertilizer distribution systems. Furthermore, fertilizer price subsidies can encourage inefficient use of fertilizer, because farmers may accept inexpensive subsidized fertilizer without making the complementary investments in improved seed, irrigation, and crop management practices needed to derive the full potential of fertilizer.

A central message emphasized in this report is that governments in Africa will not be able to tackle the problem of low fertilizer use merely by launching more fertilizer promotion schemes modeled on those implemented so many times in the past, particularly schemes that involve large-scale and indiscriminate use of fertilizer price subsidies. Whenever direct price subsidies have been used to promote fertilizer, the results have almost always been disappointing: the cost of the subsidies has been high, and the benefits generated by the incremental fertilizer use have been modest. The importance of adopting a comprehensive, multifaceted approach for promoting fertilizer was reflected in the resolutions adopted by the participants in the Africa Fertilizer Summit. These included measures to improve the supply of fertilizer (for example, elimination of duties and taxes on fertilizer, improving transport infrastructure to reduce fertilizer distribution costs, supporting strategic public-private partnerships to establish regional fertilizer procurement and distribution facilities, scaling up of input dealer networks, and providing financing to input suppliers), as well as measures to strengthen demand for fertilizer (for example, improving knowledge and skills of fertilizer users; promoting availability and use of complementary inputs such as improved seed, irrigation, and machinery; and improving access to fertilizer by poor farmers through targeted subsidies).

Another important message stressed in this report is that the use of subsidies should not be ruled out completely. When used as part of a comprehensive and multifaceted approach that seeks to tackle the underlying root causes of low profitability of fertilizer, some types of subsidies can play a useful role. Although the long-term objective of policy makers must be to support the emergence of viable private sector–led fertilizer markets, use of subsidies may be justifiable on a temporary basis to stimulate increased fertilizer use in the short run. If fertilizer subsidies are to be used, however, they should be implemented in ways that encourage the efficient uptake of fertilizer as part of an integrated package of improved crop production technologies, and they should not distort the relative price of fertilizer so as to encourage economically inefficient use. This report describes a number of "market-smart" subsidies—measures that have been used with varying degrees of success in Africa to promote increased use of fertilizer, along with complementary inputs, in ways that stimulate input market development without crowding out private investment. Examples include demonstration packs, vouchers, matching grants, and loan guarantees.

Elements of a Balanced Approach

Market-smart subsidies can be useful in the short run to address some of the problems that contribute to low fertilizer use, but unless public resources (including donor assistance) are available to support indefinitely the high fiscal and administrative costs, they do not represent a long-term solution to the problem of missing fertilizer markets. Sustainable growth in fertilizer use in Africa is unlikely to happen unless public resources can be shifted to support measures that address the many underlying structural problems affecting incentives to supply and to use fertilizer. These measures may include policy and institutional reforms, as well as public investment in infrastructure, knowledge generation and dissemination, capacity building, and improving the resource base on which African agriculture depends.

Policy reforms are needed to stimulate private investment in, and commercial financing of, the agricultural sector. Relevant options include trade policies that promote the free flow of goods, macroeconomic policies that facilitate access to foreign exchange, tax policies that do not place an undue tax burden on productive inputs, business regulatory policies that promote competition by facilitating entry and exit of firms, and land tenure policies that increase farmers' access to credit and encourage increased agricultural investment.

Institutional reforms are needed to ensure smoothly functioning commercial exchanges at all levels of the value chain. Areas needing particular attention often include development and implementation of quality controls, enactment and enforcement of contract law, prevention of excessive consolidation of market power, and creation of farmers' cooperatives and professional organizations.

Investment in infrastructure is needed to reduce fertilizer costs, increase farmers' share of output prices, and improve the reliability of service (both timeliness of delivery and maintenance of product quality). Improvement of the entire range of transportation infrastructure is fundamental to these objectives, including improvement of rural roads, major highways, railways, and ports.

Strengthening of agricultural research and extension services is needed to improve their responsiveness to the needs of farmers and to allow them to adapt with greater agility to the commercial realities of the fertilizer sector. Some rethinking about how these services are organized and funded may be necessary, including consideration of public-private partnerships. Also some realigning of the criteria used to develop fertilizer recommendations may be needed to arrive at a cost-effective balance between farmers' need for location- and farm-specific recommendations and fertilizer suppliers' need to limit product variety to realize economies of scale.

Capacity building is needed to improve the knowledge and skills of farmers and commercial actors. Training needs typically differ by cropping system, level of market development, and infrastructure. Key needs include basic literacy and numeracy, business management training, and knowledge of fertilizer products. The problem must be addressed by improved public education systems, as well as through training programs that target farmers' and traders' needs.

Improvements in the agricultural resource base are needed to help improve the quality of soil and water resources so as to increase crop responses to fertilizer and reduce the risk of crop loss. The potential public-good nature of some of these improvements suggests that governments, possibly in partnership with the private sector, might need to be involved in irrigation and water control and in soil conservation and erosion control.

The Bottom Line: Ten Guiding Principles for Public Interventions

Today more than ever, policy makers and project designers need guidance on what are the key elements of a successful fertilizer promotion strategy. Although it would be wonderful if this report could offer a general set of recommendations for designing interventions—a universally applicable "recipe for success"—unfortunately, that is not possible. Because constraints to fertilizer use tend to be context-specific, successful strategies for promoting fertilizer are numerous and varied.

At the same time, based on experience, it is possible to identify some recurring lessons that, if adapted to local circumstances and properly contextualized, can assist in the design and implementation of policies, programs, and projects that respond to particular regional, national, or subnational opportunities related to fertilizer use. The following 10 guiding principles can be used in the design and implementation of public interventions to support growth in African fertilizer use:

1. *Promote fertilizer as part of a wider strategy.* Fertilizer is not a magic bullet. Interventions designed to promote increased use of fertilizer

should be developed within the context of a wider sector strategy that recognizes the importance of supplying complementary inputs, strengthening output markets, and appropriately sequencing interventions.

2. *Favor market-based solutions.* Long-term solutions to the fertilizer problem will have to be market-based. Interventions designed to promote increased use of fertilizer should be designed to support market development and not undermine incentives for private sector investment. Where appropriate, public-private partnerships should be promoted as a first step along the road to full privatization.

3. *Promote competition.* Competition in fertilizer markets is needed to ensure good performance. Barriers to entry into fertilizer distribution should be reduced (except possibly in the very short run), and markets should be competitive to ensure the lowest-cost and best-quality service.

4. *Pay attention to demand.* Farmers' effective demand, shaped by current or potential profitability of fertilizer use, should be the ultimate driving force of input supply systems and the foundation of a sustainable fertilizer promotion strategy.

5. *Insist on economic efficiency.* Fertilizer promotion efforts should be driven by economic considerations. Interventions designed to promote increased use of fertilizer should be carried out only where fertilizer use is economically efficient.

6. *Empower farmers.* Farmers should be in the driver's seat. Interventions designed to promote increased use of fertilizer should empower farmers to make their own decisions on the most appropriate way to manage soil fertility in their particular farming context.

7. *Devise an exit strategy.* Governments should not be in the fertilizer distribution business for the long haul. Public interventions designed to promote increased use of fertilizer should be designed with a clear exit strategy, except for a few long-run public-good functions such as market regulation, infrastructural development, and research on natural resources management.

8. *Pursue regional integration.* Market size matters, so trade matters. Countries should seek regional integration and harmonization of fertilizer policies to reap economies of size and scope, which are especially important in a region such as Africa with so many small countries.

9. *Ensure sustainability.* Solutions must be designed for the long term. Interventions designed to promote increased use of fertilizer should be economically, institutionally, and environmentally sustainable.

10. *Promote pro-poor growth*. Equity considerations matter. Assuming that the previous nine guiding principles have been followed, a final consideration is that public interventions designed to promote increased use of fertilizer should also aim to promote pro-poor growth. In exceptional circumstances, poverty reduction or food security objectives may even be given precedence over efficiency and sustainability goals, if it can be determined that fertilizer interventions are a cost-effective way of addressing these problems.

What Is in the Report?

Including this Introduction, this report contains eight chapters.

Chapter 2, "Agriculture, Pro-Poor Growth, and the Role of Fertilizer," sets the stage by discussing agriculture's role in the overall economic development process and explaining why agricultural development often leads to patterns of growth that are strongly pro-poor. It explains the importance of rapidly rising fertilizer use for achieving sustained growth in agricultural productivity, emphasizes the scope of the challenge posed by declining soil fertility in Africa, and describes the role that fertilizer can play as a vehicle for addressing rural poverty and hunger.

Chapter 3, "Experience in Promoting Fertilizer Use in Africa," briefly recounts the history of fertilizer promotion efforts in Africa. Past efforts to encourage increased use of fertilizer typically featured heavy involvement by the public sector. Fertilizer importation and distribution often were carried out by government agencies or state-owned enterprises, with fertilizer prices at both the wholesale and retail levels frequently controlled and (in many cases) subsidized. Fertilizer subsidies proved costly and (in most cases) were not successful in stimulating fertilizer use. Following the implementation of structural adjustment programs during the 1980s and 1990s, use of fertilizer fell sharply in some African countries when the withdrawal of public organizations left a vacuum that was not immediately filled by private firms.

Chapter 4, "Reasons for Low Fertilizer Use in Africa," outlines the reasons for low fertilizer use in Africa. An important factor that has discouraged use of fertilizer in Africa is low profitability. In many African countries, fertilizer-price-to-output-price ratios are higher than those observed elsewhere in the developing world, reflecting the region's often difficult production environments on the one hand and its poorly developed marketing systems on the other. Financial incentives to use fertilizer in Africa are further undermined by the high variability of production, which makes investment in fertilizer especially risky.

Chapter 5, "Good Practices for Promoting Fertilizer Demand," examines factors that influence fertilizer demand and identifies entry points at which public interventions can strengthen effective demand at the farm level. Good practices for promoting increased demand for fertilizer are discussed, such as strengthening agricultural research and extension systems, improving the affordability of fertilizer, helping farmers to manage the risk associated with fertilizer use, improving the agricultural resource base, improving rural infrastructure, strengthening market information systems, protecting farmers against low and volatile output prices, promoting more effective producer organizations, and improving rural education.

Chapter 6, "Good Practices for Promoting Fertilizer Supply," examines the factors that determine the supply of fertilizer and identifies entry points for public interventions to improve fertilizer supply. Good practices for promoting increased fertilizer supply are described in some detail, such as reducing fertilizer sourcing costs, reducing fertilizer distribution costs, strengthening business finance and risk management instruments for fertilizer suppliers, and improving supply chain coordination mechanisms.

Chapter 7, "Rethinking the Role of Fertilizer Subsidies," identifies potential entry points at which public investments may be effective for fostering desirable change in a country's fertilizer sector. Innovative approaches for implementing market-smart fertilizer subsidies are described. These include vouchers, starter packs, matching grants, innovative financial instruments that reduce risk, and outsourcing of technical advisory services from public agencies to private service providers.

Chapter 8 summarizes the main points made in the report and concludes the discussion.

Notes

1. Unless otherwise noted, "Africa" refers to Sub-Saharan Africa, not including South Africa.
2. Lateritic soils are rich in oxides of iron and aluminum and are formed by deep weathering in tropical and subtropical areas.

CHAPTER 2

Agriculture, Pro-Poor Growth, and the Role of Fertilizer

Agriculture's Central Role in Pro-Poor Growth in Africa

Agriculture often serves as the "engine of growth" during the early stages of a country's economic development. Agriculture plays this role because the sector typically accounts for a high share of economic activity in developing countries and because agricultural activities tend to have powerful growth linkages with the rest of the economy. Agriculture-led growth tends to be especially pro-poor when it is fueled by productivity gains in the small-scale family farming sector and when these productivity gains result in lower prices for food staples consumed in large quantities by low-income groups (Byerlee, Diao, and Jackson 2005).

Agriculture's central role in supporting pro-poor growth has been conclusively demonstrated in many countries, especially in Asia through the Green Revolution. Although agriculture is the backbone of the rural economy in most African countries and has the potential to play a role similar to that in Asia, agricultural growth performance has been generally disappointing in Africa. In many African countries for the past 20 years, agricultural gross domestic product (GDP) per capita has risen slowly, if at all; in other countries, agricultural GDP per capita has fallen.

Figure 2.1 Index of Food Production per Capita, 1961–2004
(*1961 = 100*)

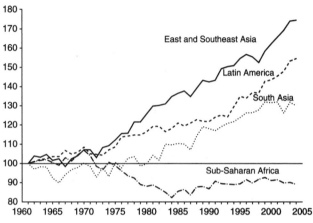

Source: FAOSTAT.

Although a downward trend in food production per capita has stabilized since 1990 (figure 2.1), only a handful of countries have experienced significant and pro-poor growth (Byerlee, Diao, and Jackson 2005).

Productivity growth in Africa, whether measured per unit of land or labor, lags far behind that in other regions of the world and is well below the growth required to meet food security and poverty reduction goals set forth in national and regional plans.[1] A few statistics on cereal production illustrate this point (figure 2.2):

- In 2000, cereal yields in Sub-Saharan Africa averaged just under 1.0 metric tons per hectare, while yields in East and Southeast Asia, Latin America, and South Asia averaged 3.4, 2.9, and 2.4 metric tons, respectively.
- Between 1980 and 2000, cereal yields in Africa grew at an average annual rate of only 0.7 percent, whereas yield growth rates in other developing regions ranged from 1.2 to 2.3 percent.

Low fertilizer use is one of the major factors explaining lagging growth in agricultural productivity in Africa relative to other regions (table 2.1). In 2002, the most recent year for which data are available, the average intensity of fertilizer use in Sub-Saharan Africa (approximately 8 kilograms per hectare) was much lower than elsewhere (for example, 78 kilograms per hectare in Latin America, 96 in East and Southeast

Figure 2.2 Cereal Yields, Developing Regions, 1960–2005

(*Average cereal yields [MT/ha]*)

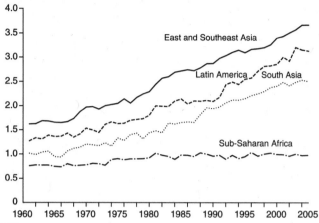

Source: FAOSTAT.
MT = metric ton; ha = hectare.

Table 2.1 Fertilizer Use Intensity and Growth by Developing Region, 1962, 1982, and 2002

	1962 Total nutrients (kg/ha)	1982 Total nutrients (kg/ha)	2002 Total nutrients (kg/ha)	Annual growth (%) 1962 to 1982	Annual growth (%) 1982 to 2002
South Asia	3	38	101	13.19	4.99
East and Southeast Asia	12	53	96	7.64	3.39
Latin America	10	43	78	7.79	3.06
Sub-Saharan Africa	1	7	8	8.71	0.93
Developing countries	6	52	102	11.26	2.32

Source: Calculated from FAOSTAT data on fertilizer consumption and land use.
kg = kilogram; ha = hectare; % = percent.

Asia, and 101 in South Asia). Even when countries and crops in similar agroecological zones are compared, the rate of fertilizer use is much lower in Africa than in other developing regions, and yields are correspondingly lower. Moreover, the intensity of fertilizer use in Africa actually fell in the 1990s (figure 2.3). In short, Africa has not yet experienced its "Green Revolution."

The low use of fertilizer and correspondingly low rates of agricultural productivity growth observed in Africa stand in marked contrast to the

Figure 2.3 Fertilizer Consumption, Developing Regions, 1970–2004

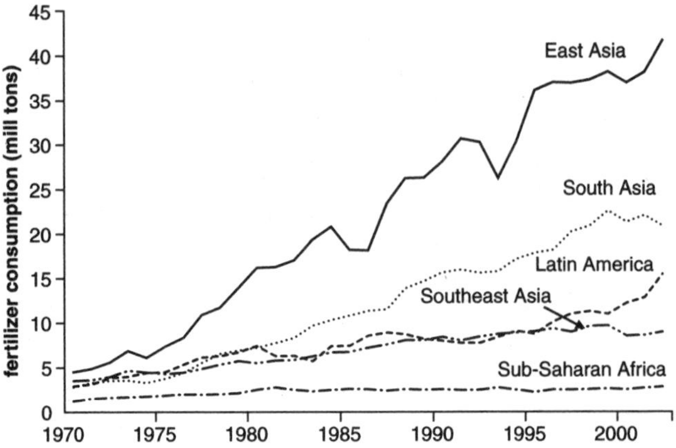

Source: FAOSTAT.

experience of other developing regions, where increased use of inorganic fertilizer has been responsible for an important share of agricultural productivity growth. Several studies have concluded that fertilizer was just as important as improved seed in fueling the Green Revolution, contributing as much as 50 percent of the yield growth in Asia (Anderson, Herdt, and Scobie 1985, 1988; Hopper 1993; Tomich, Kilby, and Johnston 1995). Other studies have found that one-third of the recent growth in cereal production worldwide has been to the result of the use of fertilizer (Bumb [1995], citing FAO). Research suggests that fertilizer could bring similar productivity gains to Africa, and indeed, strong yield growth led by improved seed and increased use of fertilizer has already been observed in some regions and among some crops, especially maize, although it was not sustained (Byerlee and Eicher 1997; Heisey and Mwangi 1997).

An Escalating Soil Fertility Crisis in Africa

The low use of fertilizer in Africa is part of a wider problem of soil degradation. African soils present inherent difficulties for agriculture (related, for example, to fertility levels, acidity, or drainage), and land-use practices during the past several decades have exacerbated those difficulties through nutrient mining by crops, nutrient leaching, and inadequate erosion control.[2]

Although Africa's relatively unfavorable natural endowment with respect to soils has long been recognized, research over the past 10–15 years has raised concerns among some observers that Africa's soil capital is deteriorating at an alarming rate. The advent of the new millennium found African policy makers facing a barrage of reports suggesting that the steady decline in Africa's soils had reached a crisis.[3] Among the concerns were the following:

- *Disappearing fallows.* Fallowing was predicted to disappear altogether in 20 African countries by 2010 and to be practiced on less than 25 percent of arable land in another 29 countries (Angé 1993).
- *Deforestation.* Deforestation in Africa was occurring at double the average rate observed in the rest of the world (FAO 2000).
- *Land degradation.* As much as two-thirds of Africa's agricultural land was estimated to be degraded (Scherr 1999; FAO 2003), mostly through human activity.

These trends have predictable consequences. Soil nutrient mining—measured in the application and removal of the major nutrients nitrogen (N), phosphorus (P), and potassium (K)—appears to be widespread in Africa. Based on a review of the case study literature, Henao and Baanante (2006) estimate that in 2002–04, as much as 85 percent of African farmland had nutrient mining rates of more than 30 kilograms per hectare of nutrients per year, and 40 percent had rates greater than 60 kilograms per hectare per year (table 2.2). If these estimates are correct, total nutrient mining could be as high as 8 million metric tons of nutrients per year across the region. Henao and Baanante conclude that about 95 million hectares in Africa have reached such a state of degradation that very substantial investments will be needed to make them productive again.

The cost of land degradation is difficult to estimate with precision, not only because data on land degradation rates are scarce but also because quantifying land degradation costs is conceptually challenging. However, a recent synthesis of studies in Ethiopia estimates that (on average) land degradation is reducing agricultural productivity by 2–3 percent per year (Yesuf et al. 2005). Land degradation probably explains why cereal yields have stagnated in Ethiopia since 1990.

Africa's land degradation problems can be attributed to many causes, but most analysts agree that a fundamental contributing factor has been the failure by most farmers to intensify agricultural production in a manner that maintains soil productivity.[4] Thus, there is widespread agreement that the improvements in soil fertility needed to stimulate agricultural productivity growth, improve food security, and raise rural incomes will

Table 2.2 Estimated Soil Nutrient Losses, African Countries, 2002–04 Cropping Seasons

Moderate/low (less than 30 kg/ha/year)		Medium (from 30 to 60 kg/ha/year)		High (more than 60 kg/ha/year)	
	kg/ha		kg/ha		kg/ha
Egypt	9	Libya	33	Tanzania	61
Mauritius	15	Swaziland	37	Mauritania	63
South Africa	23	Senegal	41	Congo, Rep. of	64
Zambia	25	Tunisia	42	Guinea	64
Morocco	27	Burkina Faso	43	Lesotho	65
Algeria	28	Benin	44	Madagascar	65
		Cameroon	44	Liberia	66
		Sierra Leone	46	Uganda	66
		Botswana	47	Congo, Dem. Rep. of	68
		Sudan	47	Kenya	68
		Togo	47	Central African Rep.	69
		Côte d'Ivoire	48	Gabon	69
		Ethiopia	49	Angola	70
		Mali	49	Gambia, The	71
		Djibouti	50	Malawi	72
		Mozambique	51	Guinea Bissau	73
		Zimbabwe	53	Namibia	73
		Niger	56	Burundi	77
		Chad	57	Rwanda	77
		Nigeria	57	Equatorial Guinea	83
		Eritrea	58	Somalia	88
		Ghana	58		

Source: Henao and Baanante 2006.
kg = kilogram; ha = hectare.

require substantial increases in fertilizer use, along with improved land husbandry practices. Although greater use of organic fertilizer is desirable as a complement to use of inorganic fertilizer, the consensus among most agronomists and soil scientists is that very few farmers in Africa can depend exclusively on organic fertilizer to maintain soil fertility levels in the face of increasingly intensive production (box 2.1). The main problem is that there are simply not enough supplies of organic fertilizer, and dwindling supplies of uncultivated land have limited the possibility of fallowing.

Trends in Fertilizer Use in Africa

During the 1960s and 1970s, fertilizer use grew as rapidly in Africa as in other developing regions. Beginning in the 1980s, fertilizer use stagnated in Africa, while other regions experienced continued steady growth.

Box 2.1

Advantages and Disadvantages of Organic and Inorganic Fertilizers

Intensive agriculture generally cannot be sustained unless nutrients are applied to the soil to replace those removed through increased crop production. Nutrients can be added in the form of organic or inorganic fertilizers (the latter are also referred to as "mineral" or "chemical" fertilizers). Commonly used organic fertilizers include animal manure, household wastes, plant materials (including crop residues), and compost made from one or more of these sources. In addition to providing nutrients, organic fertilizers contribute to soil quality by improving the structure, chemistry, and biological activity level of soil. Commonly used inorganic fertilizers include straight fertilizers containing a single nutrient—usually nitrogen (N), phosphorus (P), or potassium (K)—and compound or mixed fertilizers containing more than one of these so-called macronutrients, plus, in some cases, trace elements such as zinc or boron. For plants, the source of soil nutrients is not important. Plants absorb the nutrient in the same form, regardless of the source, organic or inorganic.

Organic and inorganic fertilizers each have advantages and disadvantages. The two main advantages of organic fertilizers are that they release nutrients gradually and that they raise soil organic matter content. There is a trade-off between these two advantages, however. On one hand, nutrients are released through decomposition of organic material, so more nutrients are available if decomposition is rapid. On the other hand, soil organic matter content is greater when more organic material is present in the soil, so improvements to soil organic matter content are favored when decomposition is slow. The advantages of organic fertilizer are offset by two main disadvantages. First, because decomposition of organic material is strongly affected by soil moisture and temperature, it cannot be controlled. This means that nutrients may be released when the plant does not need them. Second, only a limited amount of organic material is available in many regions, and because its nutrient content is low, it is generally not possible to meet crop nutrient demands through organic fertilizers alone.

The two main advantages of inorganic fertilizers are that their nutrient content is known (typically, it is comparatively high) and that they release nutrients quickly because they do not have to undergo decomposition. This means that the level and timing of nutrient uptake by the crop can be predicted reasonably well. The

(Continued)

disadvantages associated with inorganic fertilizers are their high cost, as well as the environmental damage that may result if they are managed poorly.

Most important, organic and inorganic fertilizers are only partially substitutes. The relatively high cost, combined with low agronomic efficiency, can make the use of inorganic fertilizers unprofitable in Africa. In turn, low agronomic efficiency often results from poor soil conditions, which can be remedied by the wider use of practices that add organic sources of nitrogen and improve soil conditions.

Source: Adapted from IFDC 2002.

During the 1990s, fertilizer use per hectare actually declined in about one-half of all African countries.

Today, only about 1.3 million metric tons of inorganic fertilizer are used in Africa, representing less than 1 percent of global fertilizer consumption. During 1998–2002, four countries accounted for 50 percent of all fertilizer consumption in Africa: Nigeria (14.2 percent), Zimbabwe (12.4 percent), Ethiopia (12.2 percent), and Kenya (11.2 percent).

Consistent with the region's low overall fertilizer consumption figures, the average intensity of fertilizer use in Africa remains low. Average fertilizer application rates in Africa increased from around 4 kilograms per hectare in 1970 to around 8 kilograms per hectare in 1996 and since then have remained flat. Fertilizer application rates have generally been highest in Southern Africa (16 kilograms per hectare) and East Africa (8 kilograms per hectare) and lowest in the Sudano-Sahelian zone (4 kilograms per hectare) and Central Africa (3 kilograms per hectare). Sustained growth in intensity has been most apparent in East Africa, driven mainly by intensification of maize-based cropping systems. In the Sudano-Sahelian zone, low rainfall limits crop response to increased nutrient availability, and poor transport infrastructure raises fertilizer costs, especially in landlocked countries. In Central Africa, use of fertilizer is discouraged by high prices and limited availability on the supply side and low profitability on the demand side, especially in areas in which root crops are widely grown.

The overall trends in data on fertilizer use mask considerable variability among countries, even within the same region. Table 2.3 shows fertilizer use trends in 30 African countries for which data are available (excluding South Africa) (Crawford, Jayne, and Kelly 2006). The countries are subdivided by row into those with lower versus higher fertilizer use

Table 2.3 Fertilizer Use Intensity, Selected African Countries

Fertilizer use intensity (1996–2002)	Mean fertilizer use intensity in 1996–2002 (kg/ha) and percentage increase (mean 1996–2002/mean 1990–95)	
	Small increase (<30%)	Large increase (>30%)
Low intensity (<25 kg/ha)	Angola (0.7, −69%)	Benin (17.6, +76%)
	Burkina Faso (5.9, −28%)	Botswana (11.8, +294%)
	Burundi (2.3, −6%)	Ethiopia (14.4, +71%)
	Congo, Dem. Rep. of (0.5, −47%)	Cameroon (5.9, +77%)
	Gambia, The (5.2, +15%)	Chad (4.3, +93%)
	Guinea (2.0, −4%)	Côte d'Ivoire (11.8, +53%)
	Madagascar (2.9, −8%)	Ghana (3.6, +68%)
	Mali (9.0, +7%)	Lesotho (23.2, +35%)
	Mauritania (4.0, −64%)	Mozambique (3.2, +142%)
	Niger (0.9, +5%)	Rwanda (1.8, +89%)
	Nigeria (5.6, −73%)	Senegal (13.2, +67%)
	Tanzania (4.8, −47%)	Togo (7.0, +30%)
	Zambia (8.4, −34%)	Uganda (0.6, +237%)
High intensity (>25 kg/ha)	Malawi (30.8, +9%)	Kenya (31.8, +33%)
	Swaziland (30.5, −40%)	
	Zimbabwe (48.3, +9%)	

Source: Crawford, Jayne, and Kelly 2006 (adapted from Ariga, Jayne, and Nyoro [2006]).
Note: "Fertilizer use intensity" is defined as kilograms of fertilizer applied per hectare cultivated to annual and permanent crops. "Increase in fertilizer use intensity" is defined as the percentage increase in mean fertilizer use intensity between 1990–95 and 1996–2002. Numbers in parentheses are mean fertilizer use intensity for 1996–2002 and the percentage increase in fertilizer use intensity, as defined above.
kg = kilogram; ha = hectare; % = percent.

intensity (defined as using less than 25 kilograms per hectare of fertilizer nutrients during the 1996–2002 period versus using more than 25 kilograms per hectare during that period), and they are subdivided by column into those with low versus high growth in fertilizer use intensity (defined as having recorded less than or more than a 30 percent increase in mean levels of fertilizer use between 1990–95 and 1996–2002—a period following structural adjustment, when fertilizer subsidies had been reduced in most countries). Except for four countries in East and Southern Africa (Kenya, Malawi, Swaziland, and Zimbabwe), all of the other countries remained at low levels of fertilizer intensity. Still, about one-half of the countries registered significant growth, albeit from low initial levels.

Of the four countries in which more than 25 kilograms per hectare of fertilizer were being applied at the beginning of the 1990s, three (Malawi, Swaziland, and Zimbabwe) recorded moderate or negative growth, while only one (Kenya) recorded an increase in fertilizer use of more than 30 percent. Fertilizer use in Kenya rose from a mean of roughly

180,000 metric tons per year during the 1980s to 230,000 metric tons per year during the early 1990s to more than 340,000 metric tons during 1996–2002. These gains in fertilizer use resulted from policy reforms designed to privatize the importation and distribution of fertilizer, combined with a campaign to promote efficient and appropriate dosages at the farm level (Ariga, Jayne, and Nyoro 2006). A number of other countries that started the decade with fertilizer use above the Africa-wide average also performed well, notably Benin, Côte d'Ivoire, Ethiopia, Lesotho, and Senegal. However, fertilizer use declined sharply during the same period in several other countries, including Nigeria, Tanzania, and Zambia. Major policy reforms, including currency devaluations and input subsidy removals, were major factors explaining the reduced use.

At least one encouraging point emerges from this analysis. Even though fertilizer application levels throughout Africa generally remain low, a small number of African countries achieved impressive growth in fertilizer use over the past decade or more. This growth must be sustained, increased, and expanded in geographic scope to achieve levels of productivity growth needed to significantly reduce poverty. The extent to which fertilizer use must increase is difficult to compute with precision, however, for both conceptual and practical reasons (box 2.2).

Careful analysis of the data on fertilizer use in Africa reveals another interesting point. Although it is often said that in Africa much more fertilizer is applied to high-value or export crops than to staple food crops, this is not true. Based on a study covering 12 countries that jointly accounted for 70–75 percent of fertilizer consumption in Africa during the late 1990s, FAO (2002) determined that maize was the principal crop fertilized (40 percent of consumption in the countries covered), followed by other cereals—primarily teff, barley, and wheat in Ethiopia, but also some sorghum and millet elsewhere (figure 2.4). Fruits, vegetables, and sugar cane absorbed about 15 percent of all fertilizer used. Rice, cotton, tobacco, and traditional tubers such as cassava and yams accounted for only 2–3 percent each.[5]

The relatively large share of fertilizer used on maize probably reflects some combination of (a) the relatively high fertilizer response of maize (see below); (b) strong market demand for maize, which means that maize is more of a "cash crop" than a "traditional food crop"; and (c) incentive prices for maize (in some cases). As Desai and Gandhi (1987) have argued, rapid expansion of fertilizer demand for use on cereals and other food crops will occur only if those crops become more commercialized. Their conclusion highlights the important link between increasing fertilizer demand and strengthening output markets.

Box 2.2

How Much Does Fertilizer Use Have to Increase in Africa?

Policy makers have been known to ask, "How much would fertilizer use have to increase in Africa for official agricultural production targets to be achieved?" The question is understandable, because if it were possible to specify the amount by which fertilizer use would have to increase to meet a specific production target, then it would be easier to design appropriate policies and programs to bring about that increase. Even an indicative figure would be useful.

Conceptually, it is not hard to calculate the increase in fertilizer use needed to achieve a certain specified increase in agricultural production. In practice, however, calculating the needed increase is challenging, for two main reasons.

First, it is necessary to specify an appropriate target. Before one can answer the question, "How much would fertilizer use have to increase?" one needs to be able to specify *increase for what?* Policy makers who are interested in promoting increased fertilizer use may have quite different goals in mind: accelerating agricultural GDP growth, improving national food self-sufficiency, reducing agricultural imports, increasing agricultural exports, improving nutrition and health indicators, generating employment, or raising rural incomes. Realizing these targets may require quite different strategies, with quite different implications for fertilizer use. Even if one decides on a noncontroversial goal such as attaining the NEPAD target of 6 percent annual growth in agricultural GDP, there may be problems, because agricultural GDP growth is usually some average calculated across a range of crops whose responses to increased fertilizer use may differ markedly.

Second, assuming that a target can be defined, data availability is likely to pose a major problem. Given information about (a) the area planted to individual crops, (b) the amount of fertilizer currently being applied to each crop, and (c) the response of each crop to increased application of fertilizer, it is relatively straightforward to calculate the additional amount of fertilizer needed to achieve a specified increase in production. Unfortunately, the data needed to estimate these three key parameters are rarely available. Most African countries publish official statistics on the area planted to individual crops, but these statistics are notoriously unreliable in a context where most crops are grown under rainfed conditions and the area cultivated varies significantly from year to year with fluctuations in rainfall. Accurate data on the amount of fertilizer applied to individual crops are almost never available. Data on crop response to increased application of fertilizer are frequently available, but usually they refer to crop responses under experimental conditions,

(Continued)

which may be different from crop responses in farmers' fields. In addition, any crop response parameter is grounded in a number of assumptions relating to what is happening to soil fertility levels, which crop management practices are being practiced, how fertilizer is being applied, and so forth.

In spite of these conceptual and practical challenges, several attempts have been made to estimate Africa's "nutrient deficit." FAO (2004) calculated the amount by which fertilizer use in Africa would have to increase to support the crop yield increases needed to achieve the 6 percent per year agricultural growth target set by NEPAD. The FAO study concluded that fertilizer use in Africa would have to double by 2015 to meet NEPAD's production targets. Africa's fertilizer requirements in 2015 were estimated as 2.7 million metric tons of nitrogen (N), 1.1 million metric tons of phosphorus (P_2O_5), and 0.6 million metric tons of potassium (K_2O). IFDC undertook a similar calculation and came up with figures of 4.1 million metric tons of N, 0.8 million metric tons of P_2O_5, and 1.8 million metric tons of K_2O (Julio Henao, IFDC, personal communication). Given the inconsistent quality of the data on which these calculations were based, as well as the many assumptions that had to be made, these figures must be taken with a grain of salt. Still, they illustrate the important point that although projections of Africa's fertilizer requirements are bound to vary, depending on the data used and the underlying assumptions, Africa's "nutrient deficit" is enormous, and fertilizer use will have to increase by orders of magnitude from current levels if desirable levels of production growth are to be achieved.

Figure 2.4 Fertilizer Use by Crop, Sub-Saharan Africa, Late 1990s

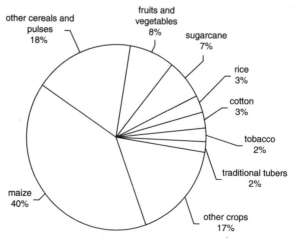

Source: Compiled by Kelly (2006), from data on 12 countries in FAO (2002).

Clarifying the Role of Fertilizer in the Overall Development Strategy

It is now widely recognized that faster agricultural productivity growth in Africa will not be stimulated without improvements in soil fertility levels (Crawford, Jayne, and Kelly 2006; FAO 2004, 2005). The United Nations (UN) Task Force on Hunger, which was convened as part of the recently completed UN Millennium Project to address hunger and poverty issues, recognized the plight of small-scale farming families—particularly in Africa—and identified improvement of soil health as one of the "key actions" needed to raise agricultural productivity and reduce hunger in rural communities.

The growing recognition of the strong link between soil fertility on the one hand and the broader agricultural development and poverty reduction agendas on the other has raised interest in exploring alternative approaches to promoting increased fertilizer use. Fueled by the rising interest in pro-poor growth, the traditional view of fertilizer as a productivity-enhancing agricultural input is being expanded. Development organizations and governments are increasingly turning to fertilizer as an instrument for achieving a wide range of diverse policy goals—not only goals that are quite clearly linked to fertilizer use, such as replenishment of soil fertility, improvement of agricultural productivity, and enhancement of food security, but also goals whose connection to fertilizer use is less obvious, such as establishment of safety nets to protect against income shocks and alleviation of poverty more generally.

The strong faith exhibited by some policy makers and development practitioners in the potential ability of fertilizer to address a wide range of economic and social problems is a bit worrisome. An important lesson emerging from recent efforts to promote increased fertilizer use in Africa is the need for much clearer thinking about how fertilizer policy fits into a country's overall development strategy. Above all, when thinking about fertilizer, there is a need to maintain a broad perspective. Although it is true that low fertilizer use is often a cause of low productivity in agriculture, low fertilizer use is usually also symptomatic of wider structural problems in the economy that limit productivity more broadly, such as poor infrastructure, weak institutions, and a lack of capacity. Unless and until these wider structural problems in the economy are addressed, treating the symptom of low fertilizer use is likely to have limited impacts.

The need to maintain a broad perspective when thinking about fertilizer cannot be overemphasized. The fact that this report focuses on fertilizer does not imply that fertilizer alone is the solution to agricultural productivity problems in Africa. Sustained productivity growth in African agriculture will depend on the capacity of Africa's farmers to combine improved land, crop, and animal husbandry practices with cost-effective use of modern inputs, including inorganic fertilizer and improved crop varieties. More generally, the ability of agriculture to generate long-term, pro-poor growth will depend on the creation of market opportunities for rural households. Although trade liberalization has succeeded in opening new markets for many of Africa's agricultural exports, internal markets remain constrained in many countries by distortional policies, cumbersome institutions, and infrastructural bottlenecks that restrict incentives to invest in agricultural production activities and depress demand for fertilizer and other inputs. And even when the underlying structural problems have been addressed, alternative instruments may offer a more cost-effective way to achieve some of these policy goals (for example, public works programs rather than schemes to promote fertilizer).

Despite these caveats, there is little doubt that increasing fertilizer use in ways that are efficient and sustainable must be a central part of any strategy to accelerate agricultural productivity growth in Africa. Yet increasing fertilizer use will not be easy. Fertilizer has a number of characteristics that affect both demand and supply, undermining the profitability of using fertilizer and selling fertilizer. These characteristics can slow the development of efficient fertilizer markets, and—in extreme cases—they can lead to outright market failure.

On the *demand side*:

- Fertilizer is a highly specialized input, the efficient use of which generally requires the use of similarly specialized complementary inputs (for example, improved varieties).
- Many consumers of fertilizer in Africa—smallholder farmers—are widely dispersed geographically, and most of them are poor.
- Especially in rainfed areas (nearly all of Africa), fertilizer consumption is highly seasonal. Most fertilizer is applied within a period of only 2–3 months.
- Also in rainfed areas, year-to-year fluctuations in rainfall patterns contribute to high interyear variability in demand for fertilizer.

On the *supply side*:

- Fertilizer is a bulky input, with relatively low value to volume, so transport costs are a relatively large share of final selling prices.
- For countries that import fertilizer (almost all African countries), the supply chain from initial manufacturing to final consumption on the

farm is long, both in distance and in time. More than six months may elapse between the initial order and the final purchase. Liquidity along the supply chain is often a constraint.

- There are considerable economies of size in international procurement and shipping of fertilizer, yet fertilizer markets in Africa are often small.
- High intra- and interyear variability in demand for fertilizer means that carryover stocks fluctuate widely, adding to working capital demands and market risks.

Because of these characteristics of fertilizer as a traded commodity, the development of fertilizer markets is a daunting challenge. However, that fertilizer markets have developed successfully in countries in other regions having similar characteristics (such as small-scale or rainfed agriculture) indicates that the challenge can be met.

Notes

1. For example, the New Partnership for Africa's Development (NEPAD) has set a target agricultural growth rate of 6 percent per annum.
2. See Buresh, Sánchez, and Calhoun (1997); FAO (2000); van der Pol (1992); Sánchez et al. (1997); Scherr (1999); Smaling, Nandwa, and Janssen (1997); Stoorvogel and Smaling (1990); UNEP (1997); Weight and Kelly (1999); and Henao and Baanante (2006).
3. Much research on African soil fertility supports the contention that a "crisis" exists, but some recent studies, while recognizing the problem, have drawn more moderate conclusions about the rate of nutrient depletion, the likely impacts of soil degradation on future productivity trends, and the quantities of fertilizer—organic and mineral—needed to develop sustainable agricultural systems; see, for example, Dalton (1996), Snapp (1998), Barbier (1999), Croisson and Anderson (1999), and Mazzucato and Niemeijer (2000).
4. See Vierich and Stoop (1990); Cleaver and Schreiber (1994); Kessler et al. (1995); Bationo, Lompo, and Koala (1998); Breman (1998); and Gruhn, Goletti, and Yudelman (2000), all cited in Mazzucato and Niemeijer (2001). See also Croisson and Anderson (1999).
5. Although the sample comprises only 12 countries, it includes the largest fertilizer consumers. Earlier studies provide estimates of comparable magnitude (Kelly 2006).

CHAPTER 3

Experience in Promoting Fertilizer Use in Africa

Historical Overview

Many African governments have tried to emulate the successes of Asia's Green Revolution in cereals by promoting seed-fertilizer technologies. Because most African countries today face a very different set of challenges than did the Asian countries when they launched their Green Revolutions several decades ago, it will not be possible to transfer the Asian model directly to Africa (Kelly and Morris 2006). Still, it is clear that fertilizer use must increase significantly if cereals productivity is to rise in Africa.

Efforts to promote increased fertilizer use have had a checkered history in Africa (for summary reviews, see Kherallah et al. [2002] and Crawford, Jayne, and Kelly [2006]). Before the mid-1980s, most of the fertilizer promotion schemes implemented in Africa featured one or more of the following characteristics:

- *State-dominated fertilizer supply.* Fertilizer imports and distribution were usually carried out by state-owned enterprises, which usually had to follow bureaucratic procurements procedures that hindered flexibility. Thirty of 39 countries surveyed by FAO in the mid-1980s followed this approach (FAO 1986).

- *Price controls.* Prices of fertilizer were usually set by government fiat. Prices were often made panterritorial and panseasonal, ostensibly so that all regions and all farmers would be treated equally.
- *Price subsidies.* Subsidies were frequently introduced to make fertilizer more affordable for farmers. Subsidies ranged from 10 to 80 percent of the full procurement cost. Overvalued exchange rates often provided an additional indirect subsidy on imported fertilizer.
- *Subsidized credit.* State and parastatal input suppliers and government-owned banks often provided credit to farmers for financing fertilizer purchases. Interest rates were usually set well below market rates and in some cases were negative in real terms.
- *Fertilizer aid.* Development organizations often provided fertilizer as aid-in-kind. Most of this fertilizer was sold to farmers at below-market prices or distributed free of charge, and the type of fertilizer supplied sometimes had little relevance to local needs.

In some cases and for brief periods, the early programs to promote fertilizer succeeded in increasing fertilizer use and boosting food production; however, in nearly all cases, the gains were not sustainable. Not only did the schemes impose an unacceptably high fiscal burden on government treasuries, but they failed to boost agricultural productivity because of chronic problems with late or insufficient delivery of fertilizer. The fertilizer that did make its way to farmers often ended up being captured by wealthy farmers who least needed assistance, rather than reaching the smallholders who were supposed to benefit; for example, see MACO, ACF, and FSRP (2002) about the experience in Zambia.

During the 1980s and 1990s, when fertilizer sectors in many African countries were privatized and liberalized, many fertilizer promotion schemes also underwent changes. Announced reforms often included removal of price controls, elimination of subsidies, and withdrawal from the market of public agencies and parastatals. The degree to which these reforms were actually implemented varied considerably. In some countries, fertilizer promotion programs continued, albeit with modifications, as when governments attempted to reduce fiscal outlays by targeting fertilizer subsidies at poorer farmers (as in Nigeria, Zambia, and Zimbabwe during the 1990s). In other countries, parastatals were shut down, and subsidies were eliminated. These reforms succeeded in reducing the fiscal and administrative costs of fertilizer promotion efforts, but the gains came at a price. Following the withdrawal of government agencies, the private sector did not step in to fill the vacuum as expected. As a result, fertilizer consumption decreased in many African countries, sometimes dramatically.

By the late 1990s, stagnating yields, declining soil fertility, and lingering food security problems had revived interest in promoting fertilizer in many African countries. Partly in response to these calls, pilot schemes were launched in several countries that featured the distribution of fertilizer without charge or at heavily subsidized prices. At the same time, perhaps in recognition of the fact that low fertilizer use is caused by many factors, efforts to promote fertilizer became increasingly eclectic and diverse. The following different entry points were targeted:

- *Technology generation.* Recognizing that generalized fertilizer application recommendations were not being adopted by many farmers, especially small-scale farmers, researchers established networks to conduct applied research designed to identify location-specific combinations of soil fertility management practices (fertilizers, erosion control, and legume intercropping) that could be adapted by farmers with different resource bases and risk preferences. For example, farmers in Malawi were invited to participate in the research, and their opinions were sought to identify "best bet" technologies.
- *Technology transfer.* Recognizing that many African farmers lacked the crop and land management skills needed to use fertilizer efficiently, nongovernmental organizations (NGOs) and some government extension services conducted large-scale programs to demonstrate the benefits that could be realized from appropriate use of fertilizer and complementary inputs (for example, the Sasakawa Global 2000 programs in several countries).
- *Input market development.* Recognizing that established small and medium-size rural traders lacked experience in marketing inputs, development organizations in Kenya began funding NGOs to provide technical product and management training for retailers willing to stock inputs.
- *Output market development.* Recognizing that farmers are more likely to borrow money to invest in fertilizer and other inputs when output markets are secure, governments and development organizations renewed efforts to interlink markets for production credit, inputs, and outputs. The vertical coordination mechanisms linking these three types of markets had in many cases become weakened following the dissolution of the colonial-era marketing parastatals.

Box 3.1

Consequences of Liberalizing Fertilizer Policies in Kenya

Fertilizer use has increased dramatically in Kenya since the fertilizer market was liberalized during the early 1990s. A nationwide study of 1,364 smallholder households surveyed periodically between the 1995/96 and 2003/04 cropping seasons by Egerton University's Tegemeo Institute shows that fertilizer use per cropped hectare rose by 35 percent during that period. Total consumption rose from a mean of roughly 180,000 metric tons per year during the 1980s, to 250,000 metric tons per year during the early 1990s, to more than 325,000 metric tons during the 2000–03 period. In the 2004/05 cropping season, the most recent year for which data are available, Kenyan farmers consumed 351,776 metric tons of fertilizer.

Growth in fertilizer consumption in Kenya is occurring on smallholder farms—it is not driven by large-scale or estate sector agriculture. The proportion of smallholder farmers using fertilizer increased from 43 percent in the 1995/96 cropping season, to 51 percent in the 1996/97 cropping season, to 65 percent in the 1999/2000 cropping season, to 69 percent in the 2003/04 cropping season. These rates varied considerably throughout the country, however, ranging from less than 10 percent of households surveyed in the drier lowland areas to more than 85 percent of smallholder farmers in Central Province and the maize surplus areas of Western Kenya. Interestingly, across the entire sample, mean fertilizer use per hectare was similar regardless of farm size, suggesting that even small-scale and poor farmers are increasingly gaining access to fertilizer.

Increased fertilizer consumption has occurred both in food crops (mainly maize and domestic horticulture) and in export crops (mainly tea, sugarcane, and coffee). Fertilizer use per hectare of maize cultivated has increased dramatically in all but the semiarid parts of the country. About 87 percent of small-scale farmers in the high-potential maize zones of Western Kenya now use fertilizer on maize, with application rates of roughly 163 kilograms per hectare, higher than rates seen in South and East Asia. The intensity of fertilizer use on maize has increased in spite of cutbacks in maize price supports by the government; however, fertilizer use remains limited in the drier regions because of low profitability.

Four main factors account for the expanded use of fertilizer by smallholder farmers in Kenya: First, since 1990, the government has pursued a relatively stable fertilizer marketing policy. After the elimination of retail price controls, import

(Continued)

licensing quotas, foreign exchange controls, and the phaseout of external fertilizer donation programs that disrupted commercial operations, Kenya has witnessed rapid investment in private fertilizer distribution networks, with more than 10 importers, 500 wholesalers, and 7,000 retailers now operating in the country. Second, and as a direct result of an increasingly dense network of fertilizer retailers operating in rural areas, the mean distance of small farmers to the nearest fertilizer retailer has declined (from 8.4 kilometers to 4.1 kilometers between 1997 and 2004). This has greatly expanded smallholder farmers' access to fertilizer, reduced transaction costs, and increased the profitability of using fertilizer. Third, fertilizer importing and wholesaling are now subject to intense competition. Pressure to cut costs and innovate in logistics has cut domestic marketing margins from US$245 to US$140 per metric ton. Despite rising world prices, farm-gate fertilizer prices in Kenya have remained roughly constant over the past 10 years, thanks to the 55 percent reduction in fertilizer marketing costs from Mombasa to western Kenya. Fourth, the relative profitability of the domestic horticulture market has raised farmers' incentives to fertilize maize intercropped with horticultural crops.

Kenya's fertilizer market reforms have been successful, but the gains are fragile and could still be reversed. Sustaining the momentum will depend on continued government commitment to supportive public investment and policy choices. Recently evidence has emerged that governance problems may be jeopardizing the sustainability of many interlinked credit-input-crop marketing programs that worked well during the 1970s and 1980s and that provided a solid commercial base for subsequent growth in other supply chains. Continued access to input credit for smallholder farmers in many parts of the country will require a strong commitment by government to limit politicization and interference by powerful interest groups. Also, investment is needed in the nation's degraded rail, road, and port infrastructure.

Kenya's experience with fertilizer market reforms shows that a sustained commitment to the development of viable commercial input delivery systems can foster an impressive private sector response that can lead to productivity gains in the smallholder farming sector and poverty alleviation.

Source: Ariga, Jayne, and Nyoro 2006.

Although they varied in strategy and tactics, each scheme had its own advantages and disadvantages (as summarized in table 3.1). A consistent theme was the effort made to scale back the role played by public agencies and parastatals in sourcing fertilizer and distributing it to farmers. In contrast to traditional models that had typically featured centralized state control of fertilizer distribution activities, most of the new initiatives assigned leading roles to private firms, NGOs, farmers' organizations, or industry trade groups. Another feature of the new initiatives was their reduced scale, which improved operational flexibility, but at the same time decreased overall coverage. This sometimes had the effect of leaving farmers in low-potential and physically remote zones without an alternative to the disbanded government input distribution programs.

Today, the situation is little improved in many places. Efforts continue to increase the role of the private sector in fertilizer marketing, but with few exceptions (Kenya is one: see box 3.1), the response from the private sector has been muted. Macroeconomic instability and high interest rates, lack of marketing skills and finance, and inadequate regulatory systems and market transparency continue to limit the active involvement of the private sector in the input distribution business in many African countries. Years of discrimination and neglect have left the private sector under-developed and input markets fragmented. The slow response from the private sector has even led to a reversal of market liberalization policies in many countries, along with the reintroduction of fertilizer subsidies in some instances. The issue of subsidies was given added impetus in 2005 with the publication of the UN Millennium Report, which advocated the use of carefully managed fertilizer subsidies targeted at highly food-insecure farmers (UN Millennium Project 2005).

The Fertilizer Subsidy Debate

In the past, many fertilizer promotion programs in Africa relied on subsidies, whose purpose was usually to reduce prices paid by farmers below the prices that would have prevailed in a free market.[1] Most African countries have implemented fertilizer subsidy schemes at some point or other, with the level of subsidy varying from quite modest (20 percent or less) to as high as 90 percent at one time in Nigeria.

Arguments in Favor of Fertilizer Subsidies

Various arguments have been advanced to justify the use of fertilizer subsidies. Most of these arguments fall into one of three main groups.

Kick-start innovation and stimulate rapid market development. This first main argument can be made at two levels:

- *Farm level.* During the early stages of adoption, fertilizer subsidies encourage farmer learning and help to offset farmers' lack of knowledge

Table 3.1 Typology of Current and Past Fertilizer Promotion Strategies, Selected African Countries

Category	Examples	Pros	Cons
State-led interlinked credit-input-output markets	Burkina Faso Kenya Mali Zambia Zimbabwe	• These markets can promote fertilizer use and farmer income growth, particularly in relatively remote areas.	• These markets are financially difficult to sustain (high fiscal costs). • Economic cost of supplying fertilizer sometimes exceeds additional value of crop produced.
Targeted government fertilizer distribution programs	Malawi Nigeria Zambia Zimbabwe	• If programs are targeted to small farmers lacking effective demand, these programs can raise productivity and contribute to poverty alleviation objectives.	• Benefits are often captured by relatively wealthy farmers (see Govereh et al. [2002] for Zambia). • Government-supplied fertilizer can crowd out private sector investment and retard development of commercial input delivery systems.
SG-2000 large-scale demonstration programs	Ethiopia Ghana Mozambique Zambia	• These programs have had demonstrable positive impact on yields, although financial profitability was mixed (Howard et al. 1999, 2000). • They have led to enduring transfer of improved farmer management practices.	• These programs have difficulty responding to "second generation" issues of input market development, rural financial markets, and stable output markets that are needed to make gains sustainable.
Outgrower company model: interlinked credit-input-output markets	Kenya (sugar, tea) Mozambique (cotton) Zambia (cotton) Zimbabwe (cotton)	• These markets have had a reasonably successful track record in improving smallholder incomes and productivity in areas where particular cash crops are viable. • They can often be used to overcome market failures in credit and input supply to increase fertilizer use on food crops for participating farmers (Govereh and Jayne 2003; Jayne, Yamano, and Nyoro 2004).	• Eligibility requirements for participation in outgrower arrangements tend to exclude participation of poor and female-headed households. • System can break down if side-selling of output is not effectively addressed or if management becomes captured by interests other than farmers.

(continued)

Table 3.1 Typology of Current and Past Fertilizer Promotion Strategies, Selected African Countries *(continued)*

Category	Examples	Pros	Cons
Starter Pack Program to provide small packages of seed and fertilizer to a large number of farmers for about 0.1 hectare	Malawi	• This program is able to put improved technology in the hands of poor farmers who otherwise would not have been able to afford these inputs. • It contributes to poverty reduction, particularly when all rural households are beneficiaries (Cromwell et al. 2001; Levy and Barahona 2002; Oygard et al. 2003).	• This program is expensive when it is designed for universal coverage. • It experiences difficulties in targeting the poorest groups lacking purchasing power to afford inputs (Mann 2003). • It erodes commercial demand of fertilizer retailers.
Facilitation of private sector investment in delivery of inputs and financial services	Kenya	• This program facilitates a long-run increase in fertilizer use based on development of importer–wholesaler–retailer networks. • Policy environment is supportive of long-run private sector investment. • Potential synergies exist between cash crop outgrower-type schemes and fertilizer use intensification on food crops.	• Fertilizer use on main food crops is constrained by problems in accessing credit for food crops. • Fertilizer use is broadly correlated with household income.

Source: Adapted from Crawford, Jayne, and Kelly (2006).

about the benefits of fertilizer (IFDC 2003; Pender, Nkonya, and Rosegrant 2004).

- *Industry level.* Fertilizer subsidies allow fertilizer manufacturers and distributors to overcome start-up costs until a market reaches a size sufficient to capture economies of scale.

This is a defensible argument for applying a temporary subsidy, provided the social benefits outweigh the costs—not only direct subsidy costs, but also administrative and other costs discussed below. Subsidies introduced for the purpose of kick-starting the market for fertilizer logically should be removed once farmers have acquired sufficient experience with fertilizers or once the market has reached a certain minimum size.

Overcome missing or imperfect markets for farmers. The second main argument is that where the private benefits of fertilizer use are less than the social benefits because of market failures, use of subsidies may be justified. In the case of fertilizer, at least two types of market failures may be relevant:

- *Financial markets.* Fertilizer subsidies can offset the effects of weak or missing financial markets if these market failures raise the cost of capital, especially for investments with long-term payoffs (such as some soil amendments) (IFDC 2003).
- *Insurance markets.* Fertilizer subsidies can offset the effects of weak or missing insurance markets, which can discourage investment in fertilizer by risk-averse farmers and discourage use of fertilizer at socially optimal levels (Donovan 2004).

Whether this argument is valid is an open question. Based on a review of six studies (five done in Asia, one in Latin America), Shalit and Binswanger (1984) found that "... risk aversion can explain only a small proportion of the gap between risk neutral and actual farm level use of fertilizer—on average around 10 percent." In any event, the existence of missing markets would justify the use of subsidies only temporarily—that is, until financial and insurance markets develop.

Correct for negative externalities. The case for fertilizer subsidies can also be based on a third main argument that there are economic costs associated with soil fertility depletion that do not enter into farmers' financial calculations. As a result, farmers use less fertilizer than the socially optimum amount. Donovan (2004) and Gladwin et al. (2002) argue that negative externalities often result from soil fertility depletion, including

- increased soil erosion and reduction in quality of downstream water supplies;
- deforestation and loss of biodiversity from expansion of cultivation into forested areas and/or marginal lands (Sánchez et al. 1997); and
- reduced carbon sequestration, which contributes to global warming.

The various economic arguments for and against fertilizer subsidies can be made in the abstract, but whether a particular fertilizer subsidy generates net benefits or net losses ultimately depends on the specifics of the situation. The desirability of implementing a given fertilizer subsidy scheme will be influenced as well by alternative courses of action that could be considered. For example, if one objective of encouraging fertilizer use is to slow soil fertility declines, it may be possible to achieve the same goal at lower cost by encouraging farmers to plant green manures. Similarly, if one objective of encouraging fertilizer use is to increase carbon sequestration, it may be more cost-effective to sequester carbon by paying farmers to maintain existing forests, as is now being initiated under global carbon financing mechanisms.

Other "economic" arguments in favor of subsidies. In addition to the three main arguments that are most often used to justify the use of fertilizer subsidies on economic grounds (described above), several other "economic" arguments can be invoked as well. For example, in a number of countries, the use of fertilizer subsidies has been justified as a way to off-set policy-induced market distortions that reduce output prices received by farmers (for example, export taxes imposed to generate government revenues, or producer price controls designed to make food affordable for urban consumers) (Idachaba 1974). Some authors have concluded that fertilizer subsidies are more efficient than output subsidies as an instrument for maintaining cheap food prices (Heisey and Norton forthcoming), but the preferred solution in these cases is to correct the original policy distortion, and this has to a large extent already been done in many African countries (Townsend 1999). Another argument that is sometimes made to support the use of fertilizer subsidies in developing countries is that fertilizer subsidies provide a way for developing countries to offset subsidies in industrialized countries that lead to unfair competition with agriculture in developing countries. Again, the appropriate response is to set output prices accordingly (for example, through an offsetting tariff), and only then if the international subsidy is expected to be phased out in the short to medium term (World Bank 2005a).

Noneconomic (welfare) arguments. Fertilizer subsidies have also been promoted for reasons that are basically noneconomic, such as reducing poverty or providing a safety net for extremely poor and vulnerable populations. To achieve noneconomic objectives, generally it is necessary to target the subsidies effectively. As discussed below, targeting is quite difficult in practice, and usually there are more efficient ways of reaching these objectives.

Arguments against Fertilizer Subsidies

Many arguments can be invoked against the use of subsidies on fertilizer.[2] Most are grounded in historical experience, in Africa and elsewhere.

- *High fiscal cost.* Fertilizer subsidy schemes tend to have extremely high fiscal costs that make them financially unsustainable, especially as market size increases. For example, in Ghana, despite relatively low fertilizer use, fertilizer subsidies made up 3.5 percent of the national agricultural budget in 1980, a figure that rose to 10.6 percent by 1988 before reforms were implemented (Donovan 1996). Fiscal costs have been the major force driving reform. Even worse, in the presence of a fiscal constraint, direct subsidies actually become counterproductive, because when governments are making large budgetary support payments to maintain direct subsidies, they are unable to finance the investments in infrastructure, research, and extension needed to develop efficient fertilizer markets. For example, Zambia's government has allocated up to 40 percent of the budget for agriculture to fertilizer subsidies in some years, which has deprived the agricultural research and extension services of a large portion of their operating budgets and made them increasingly ineffective (Ariga, Jayne, and Nyoro 2006).
- *Crowding out the private sector.* Direct subsidies that lower the prices received by suppliers of fertilizer discourage the emergence of a viable private fertilizer distribution industry, because they undermine incentives for private firms to invest in production and marketing. The policy uncertainty and instability that subsidy interventions create, along with the below-market fertilizer price, can reduce rather than promote farmers' overall access to fertilizer instead (IFDC 2003; Jayne et al. 2003).

- *Rent seeking.* Schemes that involve direct fertilizer subsidies implemented via large cash transfers from government agencies to private firms tend to be magnets for corruption and abuse. Reliable statistics on the prevalence and seriousness of rent seeking are understandably hard to come by, but casual observation suggests that many fertilizer subsidy schemes have been plagued by corruption. Incentives for corruption are particularly strong in cases where large subsidies combined with a binding fiscal constraint lead to rationing of supplies and the emergence of a parallel market for fertilizer, featuring unusually high prices.
- *Regressive distribution of benefits.* Even though it is generally acknowledged that subsidies to promote learning and offset perceived risks are needed more by small-scale farmers than by large-scale farmers (Feder and Slade 1984), small-scale farmers are rarely the ones who benefit most from fertilizer subsidies. Wealthier farmers have usually proved very adept at capturing the benefits of fertilizer subsidy programs, even when the programs are ostensibly targeted at the poor; for example, see MACO, ACF, and FSRP (2002). When fertilizer supplies are rationed because of fiscal constraints or when fertilizer is tied to credit programs, the share of the benefits captured by wealthier farmers often is even more pronounced (Ellis 1992).
- *High administrative cost.* When fertilizer subsidy schemes are administered through state procurement and distribution systems, they tend to have very high administrative costs relative to what could be achieved through the private sector. These administrative costs are separate from the fiscal costs.
- *Late delivery at the farm level.* In situations where public agencies are responsible for fertilizer distribution, and especially in cases where fiscal constraints delay the disbursement of subsidies, procurement is often delayed, with the result that fertilizer supplies reach farmers well after the optimal fertilization period (Donovan 2004). This can significantly reduce the yield effect of the fertilizer provided.
- *Inefficiency at the farm level.* Direct subsidies that lower the prices paid by farmers over the longer term lead to inefficient use of fertilizer, including substitution of crops toward those that respond best to fertilizer, and neglect of more sustainable, profitable, and promising land-use practices such as organic matter, minimum tillage, and low-input agroforestry (Donovan 2004).
- *Leakages to neighboring countries.* Because fertilizer is readily marketable, low-cost subsidized fertilizer is often exported—legally or illegally—for resale in neighboring countries where prices are higher.

Leakages to neighboring countries increase the fiscal and administrative costs of fertilizer subsidy schemes and undermine efforts to target the intended beneficiaries.

- *Creation of vested political interests.* Fertilizer subsidies are difficult to phase out. Even though fertilizer subsidy schemes are often introduced as a temporary measure (for example, to foster farmer learning or to protect an emerging fertilizer industry), once they are in place, they are difficult to eliminate because of entrenched political interests (Gulati and Narayanan 2003; Donovan 2004).
- *Lack of complementary measures.* Direct fertilizer subsidies may have limited impact when implemented as a stand-alone measure. As stressed earlier, the policy objective of promoting increased agricultural productivity through increased use of fertilizer depends on many factors in the enabling environment that together affect the incentives for applying fertilizer. Because these complementary factors are needed to achieve the policy objective, a narrow focus on using direct subsidies to reduce the price of fertilizer paid by farmers may have little impact. Indeed, the subsidies often crowd out needed expenditures in other areas.

The Bottom Line: Considerable Costs, Questionable Benefits

The weight of evidence shows that fertilizer subsidy programs tend to be fraught with economic, institutional, and political problems. Most empirical studies that have assessed the cost-effectiveness of fertilizer subsidy schemes have concluded that the considerable costs associated with subsidies outweigh the questionable benefits. Further doubt regarding the desirability of fertilizer subsidies derives from the fact that subsidies have rarely been effective in stimulating increased fertilizer use. For example, Donovan (1996) notes that even though 16 out of 29 African countries that previously featured fertilizer subsidies had reduced or eliminated those subsidies by 1994, it is very difficult to associate the reduction or elimination of subsidies with observed changes in fertilizer use, leading to the conclusion that fertilizer use is much more affected by other factors, such as inefficient marketing systems or lack of farmer knowledge. In the relatively few instances where fertilizer subsidies have been effective in stimulating increased fertilizer use (for example, in Nigeria), the increased use of fertilizer was achieved at a very high cost (Smith 1994).

Despite all the evidence suggesting that fertilizer subsidies are costly and ineffective, the conceptual appeal of subsidies remains. Perhaps more important from a policy perspective, fertilizer subsidies can have strong political appeal, particularly in countries where they have been used for some time and where farmers now view them as an entitlement. Although it is difficult to support the use of subsidies on economic grounds, realistically it must be recognized that subsidies are likely to be implemented in some African countries for the foreseeable future. Mainly for that reason, chapter 7 of this report examines some ways to promote fertilizer, using market-smart subsidies that offer some promise of overcoming some of the problems with subsidies experienced in the past. Before discussing market-smart subsidies, however, it is important to understand why fertilizer use is low in Africa (chapter 4) and to identify good practices for stimulating effective fertilizer demand and supply (chapters 5 and 6).

Notes

1. Nontechnical discussions of the objectives and arguments for fertilizer subsidies can be found in Yanggen et al. (1998); Debra (2002); Donovan (2004); Ellis (1992, chapter 6); IFDC (2003); Pender, Nkonya, and Rosegrant (2004); and Crawford, Jayne, and Kelly (2006). A thorough presentation of the theoretical arguments for fertilizer subsidies, specifically focused on West Africa, is contained in Shalit and Binswanger (1984).

2. This section draws on Crawford, Jayne, and Kelly (2006), who summarize Ellis (1992); Kherallah et al. (2002); Crawford et al. (2003); IFDC (2003); Donovan (2004); and Pender, Nkonya, and Rosegrant (2004).

CHAPTER 4

Reasons for Low Fertilizer Use in Africa

Fertilizer Incentives

Why is fertilizer use in Africa so much lower than in other regions?[1] The first and most obvious factor that could explain low fertilizer use relates to profitability. As described by Yanggen et al. (1998), the financial incentives for farmers to use fertilizer are influenced by three parameters:

- The technical response to fertilizer use, measured by the units of output (O) produced from one unit of nutrient (N) input (the O/N ratio).
- The relationship between output price and fertilizer price, expressed in units of output needed to purchase one unit of fertilizer nutrient (P_N/P_O).
- The value-cost ratio (VCR), which is simply the ratio of the technical response to fertilizer use and the nutrient/output price ratio, or $(O/N)/(P_N/P_O)$.

Some simple "rules of thumb" can be invoked in interpreting the values taken on these parameters.[2] First, using international export prices, P_N/P_O has generally ranged over the past 20 years between 2 and 3 for wheat (figure 4.1). In most countries of Asia and Latin America, and assuming no subsidies on fertilizer, the ratio currently ranges from 2.5 to

Figure 4.1 Ratio of World Nitrogen Price to World Crop Prices, 1980–2004

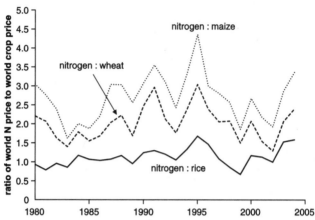

Source: Calculated from World Bank data sources.

3.5. The ratio is generally lower for rice (because rice is more expensive than wheat in global markets) and higher for maize and other coarse grains (because maize and coarse grains generally are cheaper).

Second, a widely held convention is that the VCR should be greater than 2 in a developing economy to provide incentives for fertilizer use to overcome risks and costs of capital (CIMMYT 1988). In especially risky production environments, a minimum VCR of 3 or 4 may be needed to provide sufficient incentives for adoption.

Working backward from these two rules of thumb provides a third rule: The O/N ratio for maize would have to be in the range of 7–10 or higher to provide adequate incentives to make fertilizer use attractive. Of course, these rules are simplistic both in concept (they are based on average rather than marginal productivity, for example) and in practice (they ignore many factors, such as differences in prices within a country resulting from transport costs). Nonetheless, they provide useful insights on why fertilizer use remains low in Africa.

Yanggen et al. (1998) undertook a comprehensive review of the empirical values taken on by these parameters. Based on a large number of observations across countries, these authors compared results reported for Africa with results reported for agroclimatically similar countries in other regions. (Key findings of the study are summarized in table 4.1.)

Seven "empirical regularities" emerge from the Yanggen et al. (1998) analysis:

Table 4.1 Fertilizer Incentives: Summary of Key Indicators by Crop and Region

Crop	Region	Yield response (O/N ratio)			Price incentives $(P_N/P_O$ ratio$)^a$			Value-cost ratio (VCR)		
		Median	Min.	Max.	Typical	Min.	Max.	Median	Min.	Max.
Maize	ESA	14	2	52	5–7	3.9	13.9	2.8	1.0	15.0
	WA	11	0	54	2–4	1.9	5.1	2.8	1.5	28.0
	LA	10	5	18	1–3	0.01	7.1	2.2	1.2	5.3
Rice	WA	11	7	16	2	0.2	4.5	2.4	1.6	4.0
(irrigated)	Asia	12	7.7	33.6	2.5	1.4	5	2.6	1.5	4.0
Sorghum	ESA	12	4	21	6	3.2	9.3	2.1	1.6	2.6
	WA	6	3	14	2–4	1.4	4.9	1.9	1.1	18.0
	Asia	8	2.8	21	2	1.7	2.6	NA	NA	NA
Millet	WA	7	2.8	21	NA	NA	NA	2.9	0.6	39.0
	Asia	16	3	27	NA	NA	NA	NA	<1	NA
Cotton	ESA	5	0	7	1.8	0.07	4.6	2.1	0.00	4.2
	WA	5	2	12	1.9	0.09	3.7	1.5	0.6	3.7
Groundnuts	WA	7	4	21	3	0.3	4.2	3.4	1.5	41.0
	Asia	6.5	6	17	1	0.7	1.2	NA	NA	NA
Coffee	ESA	8	5	10	NA	NA	NA	NA	NA	NA
	WA	4	2	6	NA	NA	NA	NA	NA	NA
Tea	ESA	14	8	35	NA	NA	NA	NA	NA	NA

Source: Adapted from Kelly (2006), drawing on Yanggen et al. (1998).
a. Price incentives are based on nitrogen/cereal price ratios calculated from FAOSTAT data for countries with relatively complete data series.
ESA = East and Southern Africa; WA = West Africa; LA = Latin America; NA = not available.

(1) *Comparing regions with similar agroecological conditions, crop responses in Africa (as measured by O/N ratios) are comparable to crop responses in Asia and Latin America.* This finding does not sit well with the frequent claim that soils in Africa are inherently less fertile than soils in other regions.

(2) *Crop response is substantially higher for maize and rice than for other cereals.* This finding is not surprising, given that maize and rice are usually produced in zones characterized by higher rainfall and, in the case of rice, often produced under irrigation.

(3) *Crop response varies considerably between sites and across seasons.* This finding not only emphasizes the inherent riskiness of using fertilizer but also shows that fertilizer use must be tailored to local conditions. This is especially true for sorghum and millet, which are grown in dry areas, but it is also true for maize.

(4) *Crop response is often improved by the use of complementary soil and water management practices, such as tied ridges, crop residues, and organic manure.* This is especially the case in drier regions, where the critical yield constraint is often a lack of water, rather than soil infertility per se.

(5) *For cereals, P_N/P_O ratios observed in Africa are generally higher than P_N/P_O ratios observed in other regions, often twice as high or more.* In the sample of countries examined, P_N/P_O ratios were much less favorable in East and Southern Africa (ranging from 5 to 7) than in Latin America (ranging from 1 to 3). The unfavorable P_N/P_O ratios observed in Africa reflect a number of factors, especially high transport costs for fertilizer (discussed in detail later in this chapter).

(6) *Based on the "international rule of thumb" that an O/N ratio of 7–10 should provide sufficient incentives to apply fertilizer on cereals, only maize and rice are consistently in the profitable range.* Assuming that the VCR must equal or exceed 2, fertilizer application is unprofitable even for maize and rice in some years at prevailing prices. Application of fertilizer on sorghum and millet is at best marginally profitable.

(7) *Use of fertilizer on cash crops, such as groundnuts, cotton, and tea, is often profitable, but not always.* This finding runs counter to the conventional wisdom that fertilizer use on cash crops is consistently profitable and may explain why a relatively small share of the fertilizer used in Africa is applied to cash crops.

Yanggen et al. (1998) conclude that (a) high-productivity maize and rice technologies are available, but more adaptive research and improvements in extension programs are needed to adapt them to diverse smallholder production environments; (b) the agronomic response to fertilizer in Africa is comparable to that in other regions, but the P_N/P_O ratio is among the most unfavorable in the world; and (c) for each crop/zone examined, there is risk of unprofitable fertilizer use in some years or locations.

Although world prices for fertilizer have declined in real terms and even relative to grain prices, the opposite trend is evident in Africa. Work done in the mid-1990s by Heisey and Mwangi (1997) showed that incentives to apply fertilizer to maize, as measured by the P_N/P_O ratio, had fallen over time (table 4.2). In many major maize-producing countries, the P_N/P_O is now in the range of 2–4.

The same trend is reported by Meertens (2005), who calculated VCRs for selected crops during the 1980s, 1990s, and 2000s (table 4.3). VCRs in most countries have fallen, and incentives to use fertilizer may

Table 4.2 Nitrogen : Maize Price Ratios, Selected Countries

Country/region	Period	Nitrogen : maize price ratio (median)
Tanzania	1980–85	2.6
	1995	7.0
Nigeria	1985–92	2.0
Kenya	1980–95	7.3
Malawi	1977–87	10.7
	1988–94	7.7
Zimbabwe	1980–94	6.4
Ethiopia	1983	6.4
	1992	1.9
Zambia	1971–89	3.3
	1990–94	5.4
Côte d'Ivoire	1980–92	5.4
Ghana	1982–87	2.2
	1991–94	10.2
Asia	1980–92	2.7
Latin America	1980–92	3.8

Source: Heisey and Mwangi 1997.

Table 4.3 Changes in Value-Cost Ratios (VCRs) for Major Fertilized Crops, Selected Countries of Africa, Early 1980s to Early 2000s

Country	Crop	Fertilizer/ nutrient	VCR during early 1980s	VCR in 1986	VCR during mid-1990s	VCR during early 2000s
Benin	Cotton	Compound NPK	5.1	—	2.6	3.2
Côte d'Ivoire	Rice	Urea	—	4.1	—	2.3
	Cotton	Compound NPK	—	—		2.7
Mali	Rice	Urea	6.7	—	5.7	3.3
	Cotton	Compound NPK	—	—	—	3.0
Burkina Faso	Cotton	Compound NPK	—	2.8	—	2.2
Ghana	Maize	Ammonium sulfate	6.8	—	1.5	2.2
Senegal	Groundnuts	Compound NPK	15.0	—	9.0	2.8
Ethiopia	Maize	Urea	2.7	—	9.0	2.5
Togo	Cotton	Compound NPK	—	—	2.7	3.0
Kenya	Maize	Urea	2.6	—	3.5	
Cameroon	Cotton	Compound NPK	—	4.6	—	1.7
Zimbabwe	Maize	Urea	3.1	—	2.5	2.6
Malawi	Maize	Urea	7.4	—	3.3	1.3
Nigeria	Maize	Nitrogen	7.5	—	2.1	3.1
Zambia	Maize	Nitrogen	5.2	—	3.1	1.1
Tanzania	Maize	Nitrogen	6.5	—	1.1	1.1

Source: Meertens 2005.
NPK = nitrogen, phosphorus, and potassium.

have fallen below critical levels in several countries, notably for maize in some major producers in East and Southern Africa.

These types of analysis are of course subject to many hazards. Fertilizer prices, as well as crop prices, can vary significantly across space and through time, even within the same country, and the crop price that is relevant for any given household depends on whether that household is a net seller of the crop, a net buyer, or neither. Increasingly, rural households in Africa are net buyers of cereals, which means that grain commands a higher opportunity cost price and, other things being equal, makes fertilizer use more attractive. Still, the overall downward trend in the profitability of fertilizer is fairly conclusive. What this means in practice is that unless progress can be made in reducing fertilizer prices in a sustainable way, the profitability of fertilizer use increasingly will depend on tailoring the dosage, composition, and timing of application to specific field and seasonal conditions. (We will return to this complex challenge below.)

Interestingly, in Africa the incentives to use fertilizer have eroded at a time when they have generally increased elsewhere. During 1997–2003, the ratio of nitrogen prices to wheat prices in international markets has trended downward by 1.3 percent annually, and the ratio of nitrogen prices to maize prices has trended downward by 0.9 percent (Heisey and Norton, forthcoming). Why have fertilizer prices followed a different course in Africa? Rising prices of fertilizer in Africa can be attributed to several factors (discussed below).

Removal of Subsidies

Evidence presented by Heisey and Mwangi (1997), Meertens (2005), Kherallah et al. (2002), and Heisey and Norton (forthcoming) associates rising fertilizer prices with the widespread removal of fertilizer subsidies that began during the mid-1980s in many developing countries (box 4.1). However, incentives for fertilizer use increased in some countries (for example, Ethiopia, Kenya, and Zimbabwe) either because fertilizer distribution networks became more efficient or because output prices increased under the reform programs.

In interpreting these findings, however, it is important to keep in mind two important features of fertilizer subsidy programs. First, as discussed below, in many African countries, fertilizer subsidies had become fiscally unsustainable and were imposing high economic costs, including opportunity costs associated with forgone investments in roads, railways, port facilities, warehouses, and other types of infrastructure that could have made fertilizer marketing more efficient in the longer term.

Box 4.1

Fertilizer Subsidy Reforms and Fertilizer Prices

Beginning in the mid- to late 1980s, many countries in Africa phased out fertilizer subsidies. Fertilizer prices subsequently rose, sometimes quite substantially.

For 10 African countries, Kherallah et al. (2002) showed that fertilizer-to-crop price ratios doubled for four countries (Benin, Ghana, Nigeria, and Tanzania) between the early 1980s and mid-1990s, increased by at least 50 percent in three more (Malawi, Senegal, and Zambia), and fell in the remaining three (Ethiopia, Kenya, and Zimbabwe) because fertilizer distribution became more efficient or output price increases under the reform programs more than compensated for the increased fertilizer prices.

Townsend (1999) found that 14 of 22 countries for which data were available removed subsidies and that real farm-gate prices subsequently increased in most of these countries even as world prices declined (although this includes the effects of exchange rate devaluation). Fertilizer prices increased by more than 50 percent in Ghana, Mali, Nigeria, and Tanzania. In other countries, the increase in fertilizer prices was less pronounced, and in a few countries prices actually fell.

In a review of experience in Côte d'Ivoire, Ghana, Nigeria, and Kenya from about 1971 to 2001, Heisey and Norton (forthcoming) found that nitrogen prices were below the world price for much of the early part of the period in all four countries and then moved to about double the world price in the late part of the period.

Second, in countries with high levels of subsidies, fertilizer supplies were rationed by the scarcity of fiscal resources, which meant that fertilizer was effectively unavailable to many farmers (especially the small-scale and least powerful) and which encouraged the emergence of informal "parallel" markets in which prices were frequently several times higher than official prices.

Rising World Prices

Since 2002, prices of fertilizer in international markets have trended sharply upward for a variety of reasons, including the normal cyclical patterns of investment in production capacity (figure 4.2). Higher shipping costs have also added to these increases, driven by the general boom in commodity prices and trade (in turn driven by rapidly growing Asian economies). The recent price increases can be attributed partly to rising costs of oil for transport and of natural gas for manufacturing urea, and higher energy prices may be a permanent part of the economic landscape.

Figure 4.2 Trends in Real International Fertilizer Prices, 1980–2005

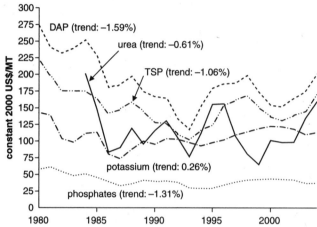

Source: Computed from World Bank data sources.
MT = metric ton.

Risk and Fertilizer Use

Given the dominance of rainfed agriculture in Africa, weather shocks are common. Weather-related uncertainty has a negative impact on farmers' incentives to use yield-enhancing inputs (or to use them at recommended levels) because this can be unprofitable in years of poor rainfall. Production variability is often high in Africa, especially in Southern Africa and in the Sahelian region, where coefficients of variation (CVs) around trend often exceed 20 percent for many commodities, compared with CVs of less than 10 percent in many Asian countries (table 4.4). Still, for many countries in Africa, the CVs around trend are within the range seen in other regions.

Yield risk is compounded by volatility and uncertainty in producer prices, both for staple foods and for export commodities. The principal underlying cause of price variability is (again) climatic shocks, compounded by weak domestic markets and lack of integration with regional and world food markets resulting from poor infrastructure and policy-related barriers. Poorly timed influxes of foreign food aid can make price volatility worse (World Bank 2006b). With weak domestic demand, high transactions costs of trade, and low tradability for some principal crops (for example, millet, sorghum, and cassava), variability in production results in sharp price movements (in other words, demand is highly inelastic) (table 4.5).

**Table 4.4 Variability in Production of Major Cereals, Selected
Countries, 1995–2004**

Country	Dominant staple	Cuddy-Della Valle index of production variability, 1995–2004
Bangladesh	Rice	5.0
Burkina Faso	Millet and sorghum	12.0
Cambodia	Rice	5.0
Cameroon	Cassava	2.0
	Maize	6.0
Chile	Wheat	11.1
Côte d'Ivoire	Rice	19.1
Egypt	Wheat	2.2
	Maize	8.9
Ethiopia	Maize	12.6
	Wheat	8.5
Ghana	Maize	11.1
India	Rice	7.0
	Wheat	5.4
Indonesia	Rice	1.6
Kenya	Maize	8.9
Madagascar	Rice	2.7
Malawi	Maize	21.6
Mali	Millet and sorghum	18.7
Mexico	Maize	3.7
Morocco	Wheat	46.3
Mozambique	Maize	11.1
Nepal	Rice	2.9
Niger	Millet and sorghum	14.2
Nigeria	Millet and sorghum	3.0
Pakistan	Wheat	5.5
Senegal	Rice	16.7
South Africa	Maize	20.3
Sudan	Millet and sorghum	24.6
Tanzania	Maize	11.2
Uganda	Maize	8.2
Vietnam	Rice	2.3
Yemen, Rep. of	Wheat	10.6
Zambia	Maize	30.6
Zimbabwe	Maize	40.9

Source: World Bank 2006d.

In about one-half of the maize-producing countries of Africa, the
coefficient of variation around trend of the maize producer price
exceeds 20 percent (figure 4.3). Twenty percent is more than twice the
level exhibited by producer prices for cereals in most Asian countries

Table 4.5 Production Variability versus Price Variability, Maize, Selected African Countries

	Ethiopia	Kenya	Malawi	Zambia
Production variability, 1995–2004				
Maize	12.6	8.9	21.6	30.6
Wholesale/retail price variability in major cities, 1994–2003				
Maize	20.6	21.6	37.5[a]	28.2[b]

Source: World Bank 2006d.
a. Measured by Cuddy-La Valle index, which closely approximates coefficient of variation around trend.
b. Retail prices. Others are wholesale prices.

Figure 4.3 Coefficient of Variation of Maize Producer Prices, 1971–2002

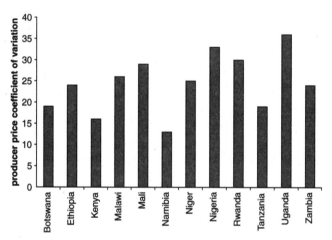

Source: World Bank 2006d.

during the period when fertilizer was being adopted rapidly. Data for particular countries, regions, and commodities reveal even more extreme price instability in Africa. Between 1996 and 2003, when world maize prices were relatively stable, the wholesale price of maize in Addis Ababa varied from only about US$50 per metric ton to nearly US$250 per metric ton. The high cost of transporting grain in and out of Ethiopia creates a wedge of about US$150 per metric ton between import and export parity.

Evidence on the effect of risk on incentives to use fertilizer is sparse in Africa. Based on a review of several studies, Binswanger and Sillers (1983) conclude that risk is unlikely to reduce fertilizer use by more than 20 percent. This conclusion was based on evidence from Asia and Latin America, however, and the analysis focused on yield risk. Dercon and Christiaensen (2005) estimated that a reduction of one standard deviation in moisture availability (for example, through supplemental irrigation) would increase fertilizer use by 43 percent in their sample of Ethiopian households, suggesting a much larger effect. Given the prevalence of significant yield and price risk in many countries of Africa and given the high level of poverty among rural producers, risk is likely to play a bigger role in Africa than in other regions in influencing fertilizer application levels. The relatively low levels of fertilizer use observed in Africa may even be quite rational when risk considerations are factored in (box 4.2).

Box 4.2

Low Fertilizer Use in Africa May Be Rational

Do African farmers act rationally when they apply low levels of fertilizer? An illustrative example using risk analysis techniques can offer useful insights into this question. In this simple example, fertilizer is treated in a generic way, so the subtleties of different nutrients inducing different marginal risk effects are missed, such as nitrogen tending to increase risk and phosphorus tending to reduce it.

A general first-order condition for optimal fertilizer intensity is

$$X = MPF \cdot P_x \cdot [(1+c)/(1-p)] \tag{1}$$

where MPF is a partial marginal product of fertilizer X; c is the cost of credit applied to input purchases (at unit price P_x), expressed as a proportion; and p is a proportional risk deduction that depends on the degree of risk aversion and riskiness of crop yield.

Assuming (for simplification) a power (Cobb-Douglas) response function with partial fertilizer response elasticity b, equation (1) for optimal fertilizer rate X can be expressed as

$$X = \exp\{\ln[(1/b) \cdot K \cdot (1+c)/(1-p)] /(b-1)\} \tag{2}$$

where K is a constant that depends on the level of the response function, P_x and the price of unit output, and other factors. For purposes of illustration, an elasticity $b = 0.2$ is used here, this being a midpoint of the values assembled by Roumasset et al. (1989), and K is set so that when $c = p = 0$, $X = 100$ kilograms per hectare, a risk-free "recommended" rate. Determining c is an empirical matter, but a reasonable value in much of Africa is 0.3 (although when formal credit is available, a value of 0.1 may be more indicative of the actual rather than the opportunity cost of credit). These two values are used in the table below.

(Continued)

The impact of risk aversion can usually best be assessed by considering any particular on-farm decision as a *marginal* additional risky prospect (Anderson 1989). Assume that initial wealth w_0, equivalent to the capitalized value of future earnings without the additional activity, is uncertain. If a marginal risky prospect is evaluated in terms of gains and losses, x relative to w_0, Anderson and Hardaker (2003) have shown that a reasonable approximation is

$$PRP_x = r_r(w_0)C[x]\{0.5ZC[x] + \rho C[w_0]\} \tag{3}$$

where PRP_x is the risk premium expressed as a proportion of $E[x]$, $C[\ ]$ is the coefficient of variation, Z is the relative size of the marginal risky prospect, approximated by $E[x]/E[w_0]$, and ρ is the correlation between w_0 and x. Here a bold simplification is made that ρ can be represented as a proportional deduction to unit marginal returns from fertilizer use, specifically assuming for the present purpose the values $Z = 1$, $\rho = 0.75$, $C[w_0] = 0.4$, and $C[x]$ at 0.1 for irrigated situations and 0.3 for dryland cases. To reduce the number of illustrative cases being considered, it is also assumed that irrigation farmers are relatively wealthy, with relative risk aversion $r_r(w_0)$ values of 1, and that the dryland farmers are less wealthy, with values of 2.

Illustrative Constrained Optimal Fertilizer Rates

Cost of funds (c)	Relative risk aversion	Coefficient of variation of yield	Cost of risk aversion (p)	Optimal fertilizer use (kg/ha)
0	0	0	0	100
0.1	1	0.1	0.035	85
0.3	1	0.1	0.035	69
0.1	2	0.3	0.270	60
0.3	2	0.3	0.270	49

Source: Anderson and Hardaker 2003.
kg = kilogram; ha = hectare.

The calculations summarized in this table show that optimal levels of fertilizer use fall very little when modest levels of risk are introduced and the cost of credit is low. However, optimal levels of fertilizer use fall considerably when credit is relatively expensive, and they fall also when production is relatively risky. When both these situations are present, as they are in much of Africa, the rates at which fertilizer should sensibly be applied fall considerably, quite apart from other factors that may serve to put a brake on use. Realistic accounting for both cost of credit and cost of risk aversion thus shows constrained optimal fertilizer levels that seem very consistent with the levels chosen by presumably rational African farmers, and these are levels much lower than rates that tend to be officially recommended.

Why Are Fertilizer Prices Higher in Africa?

Evidence presented earlier in this report suggests that fertilizer prices are generally higher in Africa than in other regions. Why is this? Several factors seem to explain why fertilizer prices in Africa are often high relative to other developing regions.

Small market size. Africa accounts for less than 1 percent of the global fertilizer market, and at the level of individual countries, the market for fertilizer is generally very small. Only in Nigeria is the amount of fertilizer marketed sufficiently large (about 500,000 metric tons per year of urea) to make local production attractive. Nigeria also has sufficiently plentiful nitrogen feedstock (from natural gas) to make domestic fertilizer production a serious economic proposition. More than one-half of the countries in Africa (table 4.6) consume less than 10,000 nutrient metric tons (about 25,000 product metric tons), the level at which fertilizer can be imported cost effectively. Because of economies of scale in production and procurement, countries using small quantities of several products pay higher prices for the product and for its shipment. In 1999, importers in Uganda were importing small lots of 500–1,000 metric tons each of various products, for which they had to pay high prices. As a result, farmers in Uganda were paying more than US$600 per metric ton for urea, at a time when urea was selling for less than US$100 per metric ton in global markets. When Ugandan importers were able to combine their import orders with those of large importers in Kenya, the retail price of urea in Uganda dropped by more than US$300 per metric ton. The high cost of fertilizer in Africa contributes to low use, but low use in turn also contributes to higher costs by making it difficult to capture economies of scale associated with fertilizer procurement and distribution.

Table 4.6 Fertilizer Use in African Countries, 2000–02 Annual Average

Fertilizer use		Number of countries
Nutrient metric tons	*Product metric tons*	
0–10,000	0–25,000	25
10,000–30,000	25,000–75,000	6
30,000–50,000	75,000–125,000	6
50,000–100,000	125,000–250,000	3
100,000–150,000	250,000–375,000	3
>150,000	>375,000	1
Total		**44**

Source: Gregory and Bumb 2006.

Unnecessary product differentiation. Africa's fertilizer markets tend to be not only small but also fragmented, and they sell many products. For example, more than 20 fertilizer products are typically available at any given time in Malawi, a small country in which annual fertilizer sales rarely reach 200,000 product metric tons. From an agronomic point of view, there is no need for such a large number of similar fertilizer products. Where specialized products are needed, harmonization of products within a region (for example, the cotton zone in West Africa) has the potential to create a large market that could benefit from economies of scale in product formulation and procurement without compromising the nutrient supply to crops.

High transport and handling costs from the port. Many countries in Africa are landlocked. They have no ocean port through which they can import fertilizer shipped by sea from distant manufacturing centers. Landlocked countries typically must absorb US$50–US$100 per metric ton in additional transport costs to have goods delivered from the nearest port to their own border and vice versa. Farmers in landlocked countries are powerfully affected by geography, because they not only end up paying higher prices for imported goods such as fertilizer but they also receive lower prices for exports, including agricultural commodities. In addition, poor roads add to transportation costs, which may constitute up to one-third of the farm-level price of fertilizer in countries such as Zambia, compared with less than 5 percent in the United States. In addition, inadequate and inefficient port infrastructure adds to costs in African countries. As shown in table 4.7, these additional costs mean that the retail price to the farmer is generally double or more the import price.

Poor dealer network. With rare exceptions (for example, Kenya, where more than 3,000 rural retailers serve the farming community), the number of agricultural inputs dealers in Africa is limited. Uganda had fewer than 100 input dealers in 2001; in 2003, even Tanzania had only 500 input dealers. Many dealers are concentrated in urban or semiurban areas, and very few are located in the rural interior near smallholders' farms. Farmers often must travel 20–30 kilometers to purchase fertilizer, seeds, and other inputs, which raises the cost of inputs to farmers, by either limiting the quantities they can afford to purchase or preventing them from purchasing any inputs at all.

Cost of finance. The fertilizer business is capital-intensive, and access to finance is an important determinant of importers' and dealers' ability to conduct their business activities. A dealer selling approximately 1,000 metric tons of fertilizer products may need US$300,000 or more to acquire

Table 4.7 Comparison of Fertilizer Procurement, Distribution, and Marketing Costs, 2003
(US$/Metric Ton)

Cost items & margins	United States US$/MT	Σ	%	Nigeria US$/MT	Σ	%	Malawi US$/MT	Σ	%	Zambia US$/MT	Σ	%	Angola US$/MT	Σ	%
FOB cost	135.00	135.00	59.57	135.00	135.00	40.16	143.00	143.00	44.50	145.00	145.00	43.50	226.00	226.00	27.29
Ocean freight	25.00	160.00	11.03	30.00	165.00	8.92	25.00	170.00	7.78	25.00	170.00	7.50	95.00	321.00	11.47
Insurance	0.08	160.08	0.04	0.10	165.10	0.03	0.10	170.10	0.03	0.10	170.10	0.03	2.00	323.00	0.24
CIF cost	160.08	160.08	70.64	165.10	165.10	49.11	170.10	170.10	52.94	170.10	170.10	51.03	323.00	323.00	39.00
LC cost	0.80	160.88	0.35	1.65	166.75	0.49	1.70	171.80	0.53	1.70	171.80	0.51	3.23	326.23	0.39
Port costs, transfer inland	4.00	164.88	1.77	21.70	188.45	6.46	7.82	179.62	2.43	17.50	189.30	5.25	98.00	424.23	11.83
Duties	0.00	164.88	0.00	12.04	200.49	3.58	1.63	181.25	0.51	1.63	190.93	0.49	48.00	472.23	5.80
Losses	1.65	166.53	0.73	3.77	204.26	1.12	1.80	183.05	0.56	1.89	192.83	0.57	0.00	472.23	0.00
Bags & bagging	0.00	166.53	0.00	15.69	219.95	4.67	0.00	183.05	0.00	0.00	192.83	0.00	0.00	472.23	0.00
Free on barge/truck	166.53	166.53	73.49	219.95	219.95	65.43	183.05	183.05	56.97	192.83	192.83	57.84	472.23	472.23	57.01
Barge/truck transport	10.00	176.53	4.41	50.00	269.95	14.87	60.00	243.05	18.67	72.00	264.83	21.60	5.00	477.23	0.60
Barge/truck unloading	4.00	180.53	1.77	0.50	270.45	0.15	0.50	243.55	0.16	0.50	265.33	0.15	0.50	477.73	0.06
Storage & loading	10.00	190.53	4.41	1.00	271.45	0.30	7.29	250.84	2.27	1.50	266.83	0.45	3.00	480.73	0.36
Interest	2.22	192.75	0.98	16.97	288.41	5.05	12.54	263.38	3.90	13.00	279.83	3.90	30.05	510.78	3.63
Wholesale cost	192.75	192.75	85.06	288.41	288.41	85.80	263.38	263.38	81.97	279.83	279.83	83.94	510.78	510.78	61.67
Importer margin	3.8	196.61	1.68	31.73	320.14	9.44	39.51	302.89	12.30	28.84	308.67	8.65	97.50	608.28	11.77
Wholesale price	196.61	196.61	86.76	320.14	320.14	95.24	302.89	302.89	94.26	308.67	308.67	92.59	608.28	608.28	73.44
Dealer cost & margin	30.00	226.61	13.24	16.01	336.15	4.76	18.44	321.33	5.74	24.69	333.36	7.41	220.00	828.28	26.56
Farmer price	226.61	226.61	100.00	336.15	336.15	100.00	321.33	321.33	100.00	333.36	333.36	100.00	828.28	828.28	100.00
Wholesale : CIF ratio	n.a.	1.20	n.a.	n.a.	1.75	n.a.	n.a.	1.55	n.a.	n.a.	1.65	n.a.	n.a.	1.58	n.a.
Retail : CIF ratio	n.a.	1.42	n.a.	n.a.	2.02	n.a.	n.a.	1.89	n.a.	n.a.	1.96	n.a.	n.a.	2.56	n.a.

Source: Gregory and Bumb 2006.

Σ = progressive accumulation of costs from the free on board (FOB) price to the farmer price. MT = metric ton. n.a. = not applicable.

inventory. The banking sector in most African countries has a limited presence in rural areas, and stringent collateral requirements make it difficult to finance business development. Importers and dealers find the collateral and other lending terms unattractive, given the seasonality of agriculture, the relatively low returns from the inputs business, and the high level of risk resulting from the vagaries of the weather.

Slow Emergence of the Private Sector

High fertilizer prices in many African countries also reflect the lack of a vibrant and competitive private sector. In addition to the factors that directly impinge on fertilizer costs, discussed above, several features of the policy environment have hindered the private sector's emergence, even in a period of market liberalization.

Unfavorable business climate. Many private firms have been reluctant to invest in fertilizer marketing in Africa because they believe that they cannot earn an attractive return on their investment. The bottom ranks of international business competitiveness tables are heavily populated with the names of African countries, which as a group tend to score poorly in business investment climate surveys relative to countries from other regions. Common problems cited by firms trying to do business in Africa include poorly defined rules of the game, weak regulatory enforcement, a proliferation of taxes and fees, cumbersome bureaucratic procedures, a general lack of security, and the widespread incidence of corruption.

Uncertain policy environment. Many policy makers in Africa think that the private sector cannot be relied upon to supply fertilizer and other inputs in a cost-effective manner. They therefore believe that the public sector should carry out these activities. Unfortunately, attempts to improve the reliability of fertilizer distribution through public interventions often have the opposite effect because government policies and programs show little consistency and frequently change in the face of shifting political winds. Arbitrary and often unpredictable government interventions in fertilizer markets produce an adverse impact at the micro level (by undermining incentives for private fertilizer dealers, both at the wholesale and at the retail level) and at the macro level (by complicating planning for the agencies and firms that import fertilizer). As in the case of liberalization of food markets, a predictable and rule-based policy environment must be the first priority for making a rapid transition to private fertilizer markets.

Weak institutional and regulatory systems. In a marketing system led by the private sector, one of the critical roles for government is to protect the interests of consumers and the general public by formulating and enforcing a legal and regulatory framework with respect to quality, standards and measures, safety in using and disposing of inputs, and business ethics. Even in African countries where fertilizer laws exist, their enforcement is generally inadequate. For example, in 2000, Nigeria experienced a serious problem with adulterated and mislabeled fertilizer products, yet regulations proved ineffective in addressing the problem (IFDC, IITA, and WARDA 2001).

Weak market information systems. Many countries lack effective market information systems to support the development of well-functioning input markets. Importers and wholesalers have limited information about regional and global fertilizer markets; dealers and farmers have even less.

For these reasons, in many parts of Africa, fertilizer is often not available when it is needed, where it is needed, and in the formulation that is needed. Even when farmers know about the benefits of fertilizer, know how to use it effectively, and have the resources to purchase it, they may not be able to find it in the market. The next two chapters look in detail at practices for strengthening fertilizer demand and supply.

Notes

1. Much of this section is based on Kelly (2006).
2. The rule-of-thumb values discussed here relate to fertilizer use on cereal crops. Somewhat different values are likely to apply to other crops.

CHAPTER 5

Good Practices for Promoting Fertilizer Demand

"Demand-pull" approaches for promoting increased fertilizer use are designed to strengthen demand for fertilizer at the farm level. In a market economy, stronger demand for fertilizer is expected to elicit an increased supply of fertilizer as profit-seeking input distributors respond to new opportunities to increase sales and income. A common demand-pull approach has been direct subsidies, which keep fertilizer prices artificially low. Given the limitations of subsidies, many African countries are seeking a wider range of instruments to strengthen fertilizer demand.

Determinants of Fertilizer Demand

To identify a wider range of instruments, it is important to understand the key factors shaping demand for fertilizer at the farm level. The three most important are (a) the potential profitability to farmers of using fertilizer, (b) the willingness of farmers to purchase fertilizer, and (c) the ability of farmers to purchase fertilizer.

Potential Profitability to Farmers of Using Fertilizer
The potential profitability of fertilizer is generally considered to be the maximum profitability possible under a given price scenario when fertilizer

is applied efficiently (that is, at the frontier of the fertilizer production function). It is determined mainly by four factors: (a) crop response to fertilizer, (b) fertilizer price, (c) prices of other inputs that substitute for or complement fertilizer, and (d) output prices (that is, the prices of crops on which fertilizer is applied). Increases or decreases in fertilizer price change the potential profitability of fertilizer and affect the quantity demanded; the change in quantity demanded depends on the price elasticity of demand, which is reflected in the slope of the demand curve. Changes in the other three factors increase or decrease the potential profitability and potential demand for fertilizer at a given fertilizer price level by shifting the demand function.

Willingness of Farmers to Purchase Fertilizer

After the potential profitability of fertilizer, the second major factor affecting demand for fertilizer is farmers' willingness to purchase fertilizer, which is a function of farmers' personal perceptions of profitability. Farmers' perceptions of fertilizer profitability (which may differ from those of researchers and extension agents) are shaped by their knowledge of fertilizer technologies, skill in using fertilizer, and capacity to evaluate potential returns to fertilizer use, given climatic and other natural risks, output price risk, perceptions of potential returns to alternate uses of available resources, personal risk preferences, and possibly other factors.

The distinction between farmers' perceptions of profitability (which shape effective demand) and researchers' and extension agents' perceptions (which shape potential demand) is important. Compared with researchers and extension personnel, farmers may perceive yield response and profitability to be substantially lower. Narrowing this gap in perceptions is one of the main challenges facing extension services promoting fertilizer. Yet a fundamental difference between farmers and researchers must be acknowledged: the farmer actually faces the risk; the researcher does not. On the research station, researchers usually command sufficient resources to ensure that the crop is planted and harvested at the appropriate time, weeded appropriately, and so forth. Farmers often face family labor and other constraints that reduce their flexibility to provide labor and other resources at the best time in the crop cycle. One advantage of conducting research trials in farmers' fields is that they better reflect the conditions actually facing the farmer.

Ability of Farmers to Purchase Fertilizer

The third major factor affecting demand for fertilizer is farmers' ability to buy it. Even if they believe that fertilizer use is profitable, farmers may be unable to purchase fertilizer because they lack cash, cannot obtain credit, or cannot obtain fertilizer locally.

Entry Points for Overcoming Weak or Ineffective Demand for Fertilizer

Figure 5.1 illustrates the questions that a policy analyst could ask to identify factors that may be depressing farm-level demand for fertilizer. The diagram also helps locate potential entry points for governments and development partners to resolve those constraints, including strengthening agricultural research and extension, improving the affordability of fertilizer, managing price and production risk, promoting more effective producer organizations, and improving the coverage and quality of rural education. The sections that follow discuss how policy reforms, institutional changes, and investments directed at these entry points can stimulate fertilizer demand. For additional details on these options, see Kelly (2006).

Strengthening Agricultural Research

Agricultural research plays a key role in strengthening fertilizer demand because a crop's response to fertilizer strongly influences the profitability of fertilizer use. Studies consistently show high returns to investments in agricultural research in developing countries (for example, see Alston et al. [2000] and Pardey and Beintema [2001]). Although public investment in agricultural research as a share of agricultural GDP has been greater in Africa than for developing countries in general (0.85 percent versus 0.62 percent in 1995), current levels are significantly below Africa's 1981 peak of 0.93 percent. Many public national agricultural research systems (NARSs) in Africa have limited capacity to carry out applied soil-management research. Rebuilding that capacity will require sustained investment in training a new generation of scientists and rebuilding research facilities that often are severely degraded or simply outdated. One strategy is to form regional partnerships to assemble a critical mass of scientists and research facilities; a promising example is the Soil Fertility Management and Policy Network in Southern Africa (box 5.1).

Figure 5.1 Identifying Sources of Weak Demand for Fertilizer

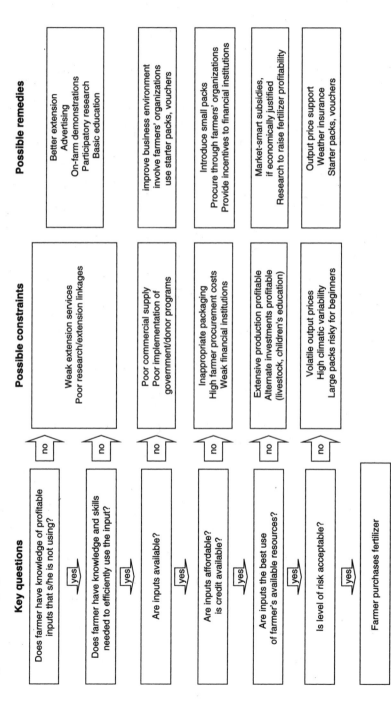

Key questions		Possible constraints	Possible remedies
Does farmer have knowledge of profitable inputs that s/he is not using?	no	Weak extension services / Poor research/extension linkages	Better extension / Advertising / On-farm demonstrations / Participatory research / Basic education
Does farmer have knowledge and skills needed to efficiently use the input?	no		
Are inputs available?	no	Poor commercial supply / Poor implementation of government/donor programs	improve business environment / involve farmers' organizations / use starter packs, vouchers
Are inputs affordable? / Is credit available?	no	Inappropriate packaging / High farmer procurement costs / Weak financial institutions	Introduce small packs / Procure through farmers' organizations / Provide incentives to financial institutions
Are inputs the best use of farmer's available resources?	no	Extensive production profitable / Alternate investments profitable (livestock, children's education)	Market-smart subsidies, if economically justified / Research to raise fertilizer profitability
Is level of risk acceptable?	no	Volatile output prices / High climatic variability / Large packs risky for beginners	Output price support / Weather insurance / Starter packs, vouchers

Farmer purchases fertilizer

Source: Adapted from Kelly, Adesina, and Gordon (2003).

Box 5.1

Soil Fert Net: An Innovative Research Partnership in Southern Africa

The Soil Fertility Management and Policy Network (Soil Fert Net) was launched in 1994 after the Rockefeller Foundation's Agricultural Sciences Program and its grantees recognized the need for better coordination of soil fertility research in Malawi and Zimbabwe. Soil Fert Net began as a technical forum to promote discussion about soil fertility issues, but it later took on new activities, including research, extension, capacity building, and policy analysis.

Objectives

The objectives of Soil Fert Net are (a) to maintain and, where possible, build up soil fertility under the constraints faced by smallholders and (b) help smallholders in Malawi, Zambia, and Zimbabwe produce higher, more sustainable, and more profitable yields from maize-based cropping systems. These objectives are pursued through the development and promotion of improved soil fertility technologies, as well as the provision of economics and policy support to help farmers access the technologies.

Membership

Soil Fert Net members include agricultural researchers and extension specialists from government research and extension institutions and universities in Malawi, Zambia, and Zimbabwe. Some links exist with similar institutions in Kenya and Mozambique. Also participating are several international research institutions, NGOs, and farmer organizations. Participation is voluntary, based on mutual benefit.

Products and Services

Soil Fert Net is an integrated, multidisciplinary network addressing soil fertility issues. It provides a range of products and services:

- On-station and on-farm assessments of promising soil fertility management technologies
- Information about "best bet" technologies for maintaining and enhancing soil fertility for smallholder maize production systems in the region
- Documentation of experiences with farmer experimentation and adoption of soil fertility technologies
- Training of researchers and farmers in new approaches to soil fertility improvement

For additional information, see http://www.soilfertnetsouthernafrica.org.

In the short run, the relatively underdeveloped private fertilizer industry in most African countries is not likely to help with fertilizer-related research, and opportunities for public-private research partnerships seem quite limited. Yet the private sector could contribute to other kinds of research that may strengthen demand for fertilizer. For example, in a number of African countries, private firms are evaluating promising varieties of horticultural crops, such as vegetables, flowers, or spices, with an eye toward overseas markets. Similarly, private seed companies are conducting research on improved varieties of field crops with commercial potential (including transgenic varieties of cotton, maize, soybeans, sunflowers, rapeseeds, and potatoes in the countries where such research is permitted). Given the commercial promise of some of these crops, the potential for developing public-private research partnerships is more promising.

These areas of research are of general interest to all farmers, but some will be more important to resource-poor farmers unable to purchase large quantities of fertilizer. To promote fertilizer use among these farmers, priority should be given to supporting research on such topics as microdosing, organic/inorganic fertilizer combinations, soil and water conservation, and conservation farming practices.

Research on crop response has too often led to blanket recommendations for fertilizer management that may be suboptimal for specific situations. Yet excessively specific recommendations may be inappropriate where farmers lack equipment to finely calibrate fertilizer applications or where the market is thin and companies cannot provide a range of formulations at affordable prices.

Research themes that can support better fertilizer use are summarized in box 5.2.

Strengthening Agricultural Extension

Research that generates information to improve fertilizer response will not generate stronger demand for fertilizer unless farmers acquire that information and act upon it. Transferring information to farmers about effective fertilizer use is complicated by the variety of technical options available. In Africa's highly heterogeneous and predominantly rainfed cropping systems, the application of fertilizer according to standardized, "one-size-fits-all" recommendations rarely results in the efficient use of fertilizer. For fertilizer use to be effective and profitable, farmers must have sufficient knowledge and skills to assess the nutrient requirements of the crop, match those requirements with available sources

Box 5.2

Research Themes Supporting Better Fertilizer Use

Applied agricultural research can improve fertilizer response and efficiency. It should be conducted in relevant circumstances so that improved fertilizer management practices can be identified for discrete recommendation domains, which are defined by agroecological factors (such as soils, climate, and topography), farmers' resource endowments (such as farm size, labor, and capital), locational features (such as access to markets, availability of agricultural services, and infrastructure), and cultural factors that affect decisions about the production and use of crops and livestock (CIMMYT 1988). New tools based on geographic information systems (GISs) facilitate the spatial analysis of data from experiments and the mapping of recommendation domains. These tools should prove beneficial in accounting for agroclimatic heterogeneity across production environments; population density; degree of agricultural intensification; crop rotations; fallowing practices; and differences in farmers' access to land, labor, capital, machinery, purchased inputs, and other resources.

Many of these areas of research have the potential to improve crop response to fertilizer and ultimately to increase fertilizer demand:

- Fine-tuning fertilizer recommendations to conform to specific combinations of crops, soil conditions, and weather conditions
- In areas where climatic risks are large, developing methods for applying reduced or staggered quantities of fertilizer with increased precision in location and timing (for example, microdosing)
- Identifying significant soil micronutrient deficiencies and developing management strategies to overcome them
- Developing soil and water conservation practices that increase crop response to inorganic fertilizer
- Developing techniques for using inorganic fertilizer in combination with organic materials
- Breeding crop varieties that respond well to increased levels of soil fertility
- Developing crop diversification practices that improve levels of soil organic matter and increase crop response to inorganic fertilizer
- Developing crop rotations that exploit the residual effects of fertilizer in the soil
- Developing low-cost soil-testing methods
- Developing fertilizer management decision tools for farmers, extension agents, and input distributors, partly through a better understanding of farmers' willingness to deal with the risk associated with fertilizer use

of nutrients, calculate the expected profitability of alternative soil fertility improvement strategies, and implement the strategy effectively.

Traditional top-down extension approaches were designed for delivering standardized fertilizer recommendations. New approaches are needed to strengthen individual farmers' capacity to make sound fertilizer management decisions. Although the appropriate mix of public-private extension services continues to be debated, at present most extension agents, public and private, are likely to need training in farm management and marketing analysis and in more participatory extension methods.

One approach that is often effective for building farmers' confidence in using fertilizer involves demonstration plots. Well-situated demonstration plots can serve multiple objectives, including research (fine-tuning recommendations to local agroclimatic conditions and farmer circumstances), extension (transferring knowledge about fertilizer management practices to farmers), and product promotion (generating demand for fertilizer among potential purchasers). The shared interests of research organizations, extension services, and private input distributors in supporting demonstration plots can create opportunities to launch public-private partnerships to promote fertilizer use. For example, private fertilizer distributors can finance demonstration plots and provide free samples while drawing on the expertise of publicly funded research and extension services for technical advice.

Demonstration plots alone are unlikely to create effective fertilizer demand. Other issues must also be addressed:

- Farmers participating in or observing the demonstrations need good training and supervision.
- Farmers require an effective distribution system to ensure timely access to seed, fertilizer, and other inputs used for the demonstrations. This distribution system must be capable of responding quickly to increased demand.
- Inputs used in the demonstration must not be excessively subsidized; farmers must be able to evaluate the potential financial returns. Some support to participating farmers may be justified—for example, if it represents in-kind payment for services, such as providing land, performing recommended practices, hosting visiting farmers, or keeping required records.
- When demonstration programs are implemented on such a large scale that significant increases in aggregate production are anticipated (which happened in some of the Sasakawa-Global 2000 demonstrations), it

may be necessary to implement measures to improve the performance of output markets to equip them to absorb increased volumes.

Because fertilizer demonstration programs do not necessarily lead to sustained increases in demand for fertilizer, they should include a monitoring and evaluation component to capture the lessons learned. These lessons should contribute to improved results in subsequent demonstration efforts.

Improving Farmers' Ability to Purchase Fertilizer

In many parts of Africa, farmers say that they would like to use fertilizer, but lack money to pay for it. As noted earlier, government- and donor-supported price subsidies have been used extensively to make fertilizer more affordable. Later chapters discuss fertilizer subsidies and measures to reduce the cost of fertilizer at the local level; we focus here on input credit and other nonsubsidy means of making fertilizer more affordable.

Innovative approaches to increase small-scale farmers' access to credit must take into account the particularities of the African production environment:

- Most farming is rainfed, making production levels highly variable. This variability is often translated into exaggerated price swings because markets are often thin and, for staples, elasticity of demand is low.
- Many fertilizer-intensive production systems have relatively large cash requirements relative to net farm income, so farmers may have difficulty raising the cash to pay for fertilizer.
- Most farming is seasonal, with only one principal growing period per year, so resources invested in fertilizer are tied up for significant amounts of time.
- Many farmers have limited collateral to secure loans, and property rights for the most important form of collateral (land) are often poorly defined.
- Institutions charged with contract enforcement and foreclosure are weak and ineffective.
- Information and administrative costs associated with the large number of relatively small credit transactions needed to finance small-scale farmers are high.

Throughout most of Africa, rural financial markets are poorly developed (for example, World Bank [2003]). In the absence of strong private financial institutions, governments and development agencies tend to step in directly. When designing interventions in support of rural finance, it is useful to keep the following guidelines in mind (for example, World Bank [2005b]):

- Consider steps to rehabilitate financial institutions with technical assistance before replacing them with new systems. For example, loan rescheduling for financial institutions may provide enough breathing space for some borrowers to make a fresh start.
- Financial intermediary loans (FILs) could be provided to viable institutions with demonstrated capacity to deliver cost-effective financial intermediation services. Where there are no currently viable financial institutions, some institutions should be allowed to participate in an FIL if they agree to an institutional development plan that includes a set of time-bound performance indicators that can be monitored.
- Subsidies to rural financial systems may be warranted, but only if they are transparent, capped, explicitly budgeted, fiscally sustainable, and economically justified. Subsidies should be aimed at building the capacity of financial intermediaries or supporting institutions (for example, supervisory authorities, regulatory bodies, and insurers).
- Subsidies to rural financial systems should be targeted in ways that foster a sustainable flow of financial services to underserved groups (such as the poor, women, and microentrepreneurs), and they should be accompanied by reforms that address problems in institutional infrastructure and financial markets.

Interventions to improve the availability of credit for buying fertilizer and other inputs need not involve direct support to financial institutions. For example, producer organizations (whose other advantages are discussed below) can be an effective channel for lending by rural financial institutions. When financial institutions deal with an organization instead of individual borrowers, the information and administrative costs of processing and collecting loans are reduced. In a number of pilot projects, development organizations have provided loan guarantees to banks to finance loans to farmers for agricultural inputs (in Mali, for example). In some cases, it may be necessary to clarify or revise legal texts concerning producer organizations so that the process of creating legally recognized organizations capable of undertaking bank loans in the formal sector is not excessively complicated. It may also be necessary to build capacity in the judicial system to enforce contracts fairly.

Another indirect strategy to finance fertilizer purchases is to make prospective borrowers more creditworthy. There is still mixed evidence on the effectiveness of reforms that permit the collateralization of small-holders' land assets to secure loans for inputs. In many parts of Africa, farmers whose claim to land is based on traditional use rights are willing to use inputs and to make productivity-enhancing investments whose benefits accrue over time. Efforts to provide land titles and legalize land markets therefore are unlikely to increase demand for fertilizer per se, although they may improve access to credit in the long run.

A third indirect strategy to finance fertilizer purchases involves collat-eralizing farm output. Many of the more successful input credit programs in Africa (judged by credit volume and repayment rates) have used crops as collateral for input loans (examples include vertically integrated cotton, coffee, tea, and sugar production systems and outgrower schemes for tobacco and horticultural crops). Because the input credit programs have often been part of a larger parastatal system that has been characterized by inefficiencies in processing or export marketing, frequently there has been pressure to privatize the entire system, with inadequate attention to the potential disruption to the input credit component. Experience with liberalizing and privatizing the cotton sectors in Ghana and Uganda and the coffee sector in Tanzania, for example, indicates that reforms can have a significant negative impact on fertilizer demand if alternative institutions for securing input credit are not developed (Poulton, Dorward, and Kydd 1998; Kelly, Adesina, and Gordon 2003; Poulton et al. 2004).

Yet collateralizing farm output can work (for example, World Bank [2005c]). The warehouse receipt program for maize in Zambia and the rice credit storage program in Mali are innovative approaches that col-lateralize farmers' production without relying on vertically integrated production and marketing systems. These programs allow farmers to use stored production as collateral. By borrowing against stored grain, farmers are able to cover postharvest consumption expenditures by using short-term credit, rather than by selling production while output prices are low.

This discussion has focused on providing credit to farmers for fertilizer purchases, but it is important to remember that even in the absence of credit, it may be possible to overcome a lack of purchasing power. In Kenya, the Sustainable Community-Oriented Development Programme (SCODP) has stimulated fertilizer adoption among some of the nation's poorest farmers by combining research to identify recommendations that use fertilizer more efficiently with marketing efforts to sell improved seed and fertilizer in small packages (Seward and Okello 1999). There is also good evidence that nonfarm income represents an important share of rural household income in Africa and is often used to purchase inputs, which suggests that programs that create employment in rural areas can help farmers overcome liquidity constraints. Noncredit approaches are especially relevant for resource-poor farmers in zones where small amounts of fertilizer can overcome a highly constraining nutrient or micronutrient soil deficiency, but will not stimulate sizable increases in aggregate fertilizer demand.

Managing Price Risk

When output prices fluctuate widely across seasons and years, farmers have difficulty assessing the potential benefits of fertilizer, which may result in suboptimal use. Extreme price fluctuations can also increase the severity of losses in years of surplus production, when prices drop precipitously, and risk-averse farmers reduce purchases of fertilizer and other inputs to limit their exposure to possible losses and potential credit default. One way to protect farmers against the effects of low output prices is to ensure that technical change (usually associated with increased use of purchased inputs, including fertilizer and drought-tolerant varieties) proceeds rapidly enough for farm-level productivity gains to outpace the decline in output prices. When this happens, farmers enjoy increased earnings even as real prices paid by consumers to purchase food fall. Because such technical change has been slow in Africa, governments have resorted to a variety of policy options.

During the 1970s, many African governments responded to low and unstable output prices by intervening directly in markets. One or more government agencies or parastatals would purchase a crop and resell it on the domestic market (in the case of food crops) or the international market (in the case of export crops). The fiscal burden of supporting the subsidies in combination with the highly inefficient marketing agencies eventually exceeded governments' capacity to continue the price stabilization and support programs (Jayne and Jones 1997). Beginning in the 1980s, donors and international lending agencies began promoting food-marketing and food-price policy reform in Africa to stem the rising costs of price stabilization policies. Reform recommendations included liberalizing food markets and reducing government purchasing and selling, reforming commercial codes to make them more business-friendly, and relying on trade—rather than management of government stocks—to address temporary supply imbalances.

Good market information is crucial if these types of policy reforms are to yield the anticipated results. Government investments to improve the quality and availability of market information, coupled with extension investments to improve farmers' skills in using this type of information, can contribute to better decision making in fertilizer purchases and reduce price volatility in output markets.

Governments in several African countries have attempted to capitalize on the revolution in information and communications technology by introducing market information systems to serve the agricultural community. These initiatives have had mixed results. Market information has public-good elements, but many early initiatives to develop public sector market information systems failed, often because the systems lacked commercial utility and were unsustainable (Robbins 2000; Shepherd 1997). More recently, some success stories have started to emerge, suggesting that earlier problems are being overcome with the benefit of experience (see box 5.3). Building sustainable market information systems will require identifying mechanisms for private management; obtaining at least partial cost recovery; having a modest scope (covering only commercially important commodities); ensuring a participatory process, with users defining their needs; including some nonprice data (market closures, quality assessments, and food safety problems); and making cost-effective use of available information technologies to achieve timely and wide dissemination.

There is general agreement that the postreform environment continues to expose both farmers and consumers to significant food price instability and risk. In light of evidence that food price stabilization generally has not worked and may actually have worsened price instability in many countries, a consensus is emerging around the need for increased long-term public investment in goods and services that can reduce price instability, as well as the production instability that contributes to it (World Bank 2006c).

Managing Production Risk

Farmers in Africa use many strategies to deal with production risks: information gathering, risk avoidance, diversification of income sources, and "social banking," which includes a variety of informal risk-pooling arrangements with friends and family.

What can be done to help farmers manage risks associated with fertilizer? To begin with, governments can implement policies that reinforce and strengthen the traditional risk management strategies listed above (for example, by disseminating market information, publicizing new

Box 5.3

"Silicon Mali"

Mali's success in establishing a market information system earned it the title of "Silicon Mali" by *Forbes Magazine* in 2002. Mali's market information system (*Observatoire des Marchés Agricoles*) is powered by enumerators who visit 58 markets located all over the country and record prices and product flows for selected grains, crops, and livestock. The information is entered into laptop computers and e-mailed by FM radio waves on solar-powered equipment to regional offices, where the data are compiled and used in the preparation of reports targeted to different types of producers and traders.

Built up over the course of a decade, the system has made Malian grain farmers more efficient because they can easily determine when and where to sell their products and for what price. Armed with better information, the government can now rely on the private sector to shift surpluses to areas with shortages without resorting to foreign aid. Mali's information system has become a model for the rest of West Africa, and countries like Niger and Burkina Faso are setting up similar systems that will be linked together. Soon, farmers will be able to do more selling across national boundaries.

Another recent innovation is reduced reliance on donor funding. The operating costs of the system are now covered entirely by Malian government funding, supplemented by small amounts of income from sales of services for specialized data products and analyses. Some capital costs continue to be covered by donors.

Source: Sansoni 2002.

technologies, and encouraging income diversification). In addition, they can support the development of formal risk management instruments that protect farmers from production risk. Some of these could certainly be provided through private financial institutions and producer organizations, whereas others are likely to require public support.

Experience from other developing regions suggests that formal risk management instruments will grow in popularity in Africa as agriculture becomes increasingly commercial. Over the longer term, the goal must be to develop a selection of instruments adapted to the wide range of technical, economic, and social constraints faced by African farmers. Private financial institutions should be encouraged to develop instruments to deal with risks that are frequent and systemic, although not catastrophic.

Weather-indexed insurance, already well established in India and now being piloted in Ethiopia, Malawi, and other African countries, is a new instrument for reducing the risk of weather-induced production variability (box 5.4). Instead of issuing policies that pay out depending on the performance of crops grown by individual farmers, insurers issue policies that pay out depending on a readily measured, objectively

Box 5.4

Insurance Protects Producers from Drought in India

A World Bank–assisted pilot project helped to launch India's first rainfall insurance program. The project demonstrated that weather-indexed insurance could benefit farmers and could avoid the problems of moral hazard and high administrative costs associated with traditional crop insurance programs. Under the project, a local bank sold policies to producers, with the premium and maximum liability varying by scale. For example, farms between 0.8 and 2 hectares paid 600 rupees (Rs), with a maximum liability of Rs 20,000. The payout structure was based on rainfall. It weighted rainfall deficiencies in the more critical periods for plant growth more heavily than deficiencies in other periods.

Following the pilot project, one of India's largest microfinance institutions began to offer rainfall insurance. The local bank offers policies to its borrowers, as well as to outside clients (such as members of women's self-help groups), and it hopes to lower the interest rate for borrowers based on the reduced risk of default. Lessons include the following:

• The index must be based on long-term statistical information and credible actuarial models. To this end, the public sector can develop information sources such as risk maps.

• The trigger (the event or circumstance that permits the policy holder to claim payment) must be an unambiguous threshold of a quantifiable variable over which farmers have no control.

• The payment schedule must be clear, quantifiable, and monitored by an independent third party.

• Education programs and technical assistance for stakeholders should be provided.

• Combining index-based programs with other types of insurance and financial services can improve the effectiveness of the trigger.

Source: Hess 2003.

verifiable index—for example, rainfall in a specified area. Reliance on nondiscretionary and objectively verifiable indicators can substantially reduce opportunities to misrepresent crop losses and gain unjustified compensation. Implementation challenges still need to be overcome. Many regions lack reliable rainfall and yield data; even if data are available, there must be strong correlations between typical on-farm yields and rainfall levels. Either weather-indexed insurance can be sold as an optional policy that farmers can choose to purchase, or it can be offered as an obligatory complement to fertilizer loans and set at a level that will ensure sufficient cash payout to cover the loan in the event of unfavorable weather. Weather-indexed insurance represents an attractive option in medium-potential areas where fertilizer use is (on average) profitable, but where there is moderate risk of drought causing high losses. It is less appropriate for very dry areas, in part because the frequency of drought would require a high insurance premium and in part because fertilizer may not be very profitable on average.

Governments must devote more attention to developing mechanisms that protect farmers from, or allow them to recover from, catastrophic risks, but without setting the stage for future problems. For example, governments and aid agencies have distributed free seed and fertilizer to farmers after droughts, floods, or locust attacks, yet this strategy can undermine private input markets, making it even more difficult for farmers to obtain inputs in subsequent years. Distribution of vouchers that can be redeemed for seed or fertilizer might help farmers recover from disasters and help build demand for inputs from private distributors.

Another strategy for reducing production risk is to improve the resource base on which agriculture depends. To the extent that Africa's often harsh physical environments can be made more hospitable for agriculture, agriculture will become more profitable, and demand for agricultural inputs, including fertilizer, will grow. Governments can make investments—and through well-designed policies, they can encourage farmers to make investments—to mitigate adverse impacts on the agricultural resource base and increase the profitability of agriculture. Soil and water conservation structures and irrigation systems are examples of such investments.

Soil and water conservation structures. Soil and water conservation (SWC) structures can significantly improve the productivity and incomes of farmers in rainfed production systems, and they can play an important role in making fertilizer use more efficient and more profitable. For example, three years after the introduction of SWC practices in a cotton-producing village of Mali, sorghum yields were 57 percent higher than in the base year, millet yields 48 percent higher, maize yields 85 percent higher, and cotton yields 23 percent higher, while rainfall the third year was much lower (only 69 percent of the base year's rainfall) (Berthé 2004). Antierosion structures, such as contour ridges or rock lines, vegetative bands, and living hedges, slow down soil degradation and conserve moisture. Often they are used in conjunction with practices to retain soil moisture (planting holes known as *zai* and composting). Investments in SWC structures provide substantial benefits to individual farmers, but they also contribute to community welfare by raising water tables (which may increase opportunities for dry-season farming), limiting deforestation arising from extensive production practices, and reducing silting in rivers.

Adoption of SWC technologies in most African countries has not gone beyond a small group of relatively well-off farmers, who have demonstrated the yield-increasing and risk-reducing potential. Governments now must assess the potential costs and benefits of public investments to promote adoption among farmers who are less well-off. Public investments could support extension specialists to train farmers, provide equipment and technicians to mark contours, and supply vehicles to transport materials such as rocks and plants. Although the likely increase in fertilizer use and productivity per hectare are both relatively small compared with those that would be realized from constructing full-fledged irrigation systems, the level of investment is much lower. More important, the aggregate impact on productivity and poverty reduction could be much greater than that derived from irrigation, given the large number of African farmers who work in rainfed production systems.

Irrigation systems. Compared with other regions of the world, Africa has a much lower proportion of irrigated farmland. The public-good character of large-scale irrigation investments is generally recognized, and therefore the producers who benefit from these investments are rarely asked to contribute to the costs of building the initial infrastructure. This is in sharp contrast to programs promoting the adoption of SWC practices where farmers are generally required to support the full costs even if there are social and environmental benefits such as reduced poverty and less erosion and silting of rivers. Although current development plans call for significantly greater irrigation investment, the challenge is to make such investment cost-effective. Large-scale irrigation schemes have not always lived up to expectations in technical, economic, environmental, and social terms. Medium-scale and especially small-scale irrigation schemes generally show much greater promise because the initial investment costs are usually lower (meaning that a greater proportion can be shared by the beneficiaries) and because responsibility for water management in medium- and small-scale systems can often be transferred to users, rather than left to a centralized authority (World Bank 2006b).

Promoting Farmer Empowerment and Producer Organizations

Most African farmers are smallholders who lack the economic and political power to capture economies of scale in input procurement, production, processing, storage, and marketing. For many, the easiest way to acquire such power is by joining with others in a producer organization. Strong producer organizations can improve the competitiveness and welfare of small-scale farmers while serving as a social safety net.

Producer organizations do not appear spontaneously; they usually require public support and nurturing. Initial requirements include the establishment of an enabling policy environment, a facilitating legal framework, and a regulatory climate conducive to business. Additional public support is often needed to help producer associations become established and to overcome obstacles linked to their members' lack of formal education, business management experience, and physical and financial resources. As farmers become more "market-savvy," the potential benefits of collective action become more apparent, and their interest in participating in producer organizations tends to increase.

Effective producer organizations can play multiple roles in building demand for fertilizer. They can

- increase members' market power, allowing them to secure more favorable input or output prices;
- reduce marketing costs for fertilizer and other inputs, as well as marketing costs for outputs, by allowing members to engage in collective storage and transport;
- improve communications with research and extension services;
- allow members to access credit; and
- help members advocate for producer-friendly policies.

Several lessons have emerged from the experience with producer organizations in Africa and elsewhere (Bingen, Serrano, and Howard 2003, Coulter et al. 1999, Stringfellow et al. 1997). Earlier programs to support producer organizations focused on promoting technology, rather than developing human capacity. Farmer organizations (for example, cotton producer organizations and coffee producer organizations) formed exclusively in response to a major subsector development program often have been endowed with insufficient management skills and invested with limited decision-making power, leaving members ill equipped to make critical decisions about input use or output marketing strategies. Rarely has there been time to build the leadership and management capacity to avoid such problems as side-selling or capture by an elite, which can lead to credit defaults and program failure. Conflicts of interest have also arisen when training for farmer management and advocacy skills has been provided by organizations (parastatals, private firms, or NGOs) whose own interests are not always well served by the creation of strong, independent producer associations.

Increasing Investment in Rural Education
Currently only about 55 percent of eligible children in Africa complete primary school. In many African countries, rates of primary school attendance and completion are much higher for boys than for girls, and they are much higher in urban than in rural areas.

Low rates of primary school attendance have direct implications for agriculture. When literacy levels are low, the cost of agricultural extension rises and the breadth of coverage decreases because extension agents must interact directly with farmers to provide technical information, rather than relying on printed materials. The particularly low schooling rates for girls observed in many African countries hamper efforts to transfer improved technologies to women farmers and to transmit nutrition and health information, which are important determinants of the quality of the overall household labor supply.

Unfortunately, investment in rural primary education offers no "quick fix" for low productivity in agriculture. Adult education programs may be needed to support training in the increasingly knowledge-intensive fertilizer practices recommended for Africa. In Mali, adult literacy training in local languages was followed with training to apply newly acquired literacy skills to crop and resource management problems, and financial institutions were required to accept loan applications in local languages. Positive impacts of adult literacy programs have been observed in the use of production credit, acquisition of inputs (including fertilizer), farm-level productivity and profitability, and participation in producer organizations.

Balancing Short- and Long-Term Interventions

This review of good practices for promoting fertilizer demand has identified a wide range of policy and investment options. In designing fertilizer promotion programs, it is important to maintain a balance between interventions that have the potential to increase fertilizer consumption rapidly in the short run (such as direct price or credit subsidies, and demonstration programs) and interventions that are needed to ensure long-term sustainable growth in consumption (such as improved institutions for quality control, contract enforcement, market information, and risk sharing; generation and extension of more cost-effective and less risky fertilizer technologies; and training farmers in literacy and other skills needed to create and manage viable farmer organizations). An increased sense of urgency about reducing rural poverty to meet the Millennium Development Goals is putting intense pressure on governments and development partners to invest heavily in the short-term strategies, yet sustainable rates of poverty reduction based on agricultural productivity growth through the use of improved inputs such as fertilizers will require a balanced approach.

CHAPTER 6

Good Practices for Promoting Fertilizer Supply

Determinants of Input Supply

"Supply-push" approaches for promoting increased fertilizer use are designed to improve the availability and affordability of fertilizer in the market. They focus on policy reforms, institutional changes, and supporting investments that can make fertilizer production and distribution more profitable. In the short run, increased profitability will encourage suppliers to offer more fertilizer at the prevailing market price. Over the long run, sustained high profitability will draw new firms into the market, increasing supplies.

In competitive markets, prices are determined through transactions negotiated among many sellers and buyers. In such markets, individual firms cannot influence prices, so their profits depend on the size of their costs. For this reason, many supply-push approaches focus on opportunities to reduce the costs associated with fertilizer production, procurement, and distribution. The costs of supplying fertilizer are determined by four main factors: (a) sourcing costs, (b) distribution costs, (c) the availability and cost of business finance and risk management instruments, and (d) the adequacy of supply chain coordination mechanisms.

Entry Points for Overcoming Weak or Ineffective Supply of Fertilizer

Figure 6.1 illustrates the questions that a policy analyst could ask to identify factors that may be depressing the supply of fertilizer. The diagram also helps locate binding constraints that discourage procurement (through manufacturing or importation) and distribution of fertilizer, as well as potential entry points for governments and development partners to resolve those constraints. Entry points with the greatest potential for stimulating fertilizer supply include those related to (a) reducing fertilizer sourcing costs, (b) reducing fertilizer distribution costs, (c) improving the environment for business financing and risk management, and (d) improving the environment for supply chain coordination. The sections that follow discuss how policy reforms, institutional changes, and investments directed at these entry points can reduce costs and increase profits at various levels of the supply chain. (For additional details on these issues, see Gregory and Bumb [2006].)

Reducing Fertilizer Sourcing Costs

High fertilizer sourcing costs reduce the profitability of distributing fertilizer and discourage increased supply. More than 90 percent of the fertilizer used in Africa is imported. Until African fertilizer markets become large enough to justify investment in large-scale production facilities, importing will be the most cost-effective strategy. Fortunately, fertilizer products are readily available in global markets, so African countries can continue to depend on imports without incurring a significant disadvantage. The keys are addressing the constraints that increase import costs and remaining cognizant of the fact that, as markets grow in size, the opportunities for cost-effective sourcing will change and (in some cases) may include domestic production.

Reducing Fertilizer Import Costs. In the 2002/03 cropping season, Africa imported nearly 1.4 million metric tons of fertilizer. The volume of fertilizer imports has increased steadily over the years, with some year-to-year variability caused mainly by weather-induced fluctuations in demand (figure 6.2). The significant cost savings that can be realized when fertilizer is imported in bulk are rarely captured in Africa. Constraints to bulk importing and associated opportunities to achieve cost savings are discussed in the following sections.

Figure 6.1 Identifying Causes of Inadequate Supply of Fertilizer

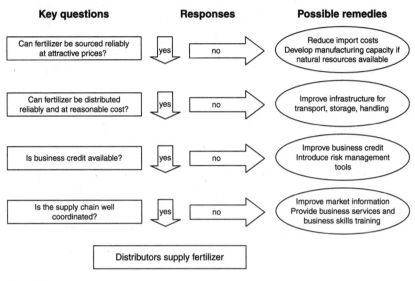

Source: Authors.

Improving Access to Foreign Exchange and Credit. International prices for fertilizer are normally quoted in U.S. dollars, and transactions require U.S. dollar payment, usually made using irrevocable letters of credit. Importing fertilizer requires short-term financing in large amounts (at current prices, for example, US$5 million in credit over two to three months is needed to import 25,000 metric tons of urea), and letters of credit must often be covered by 100 percent collateral. Cumbersome procedures for securing large-scale financing limit prospective importers' response time and flexibility in negotiating with sellers and reduce the attractiveness of transactions to overseas sellers. Consequently, African buyers are often unable to place fertilizer orders when prices are lowest.

Several strategies can facilitate access to credit to purchase fertilizer:

- Promote collaboration among fertilizer importers, with the objective of getting them to pool financial resources to increase their creditworthiness.
- Combine purchasing power to allow importers to qualify for export trade credits from governments that are seeking to expand their fertilizer industries.
- Identify flexible sources of credit. Donor lending has been used to support fertilizer import credits in some countries.

Figure 6.2 Fertilizer Imports, Sub-Saharan Africa, 1962–2002

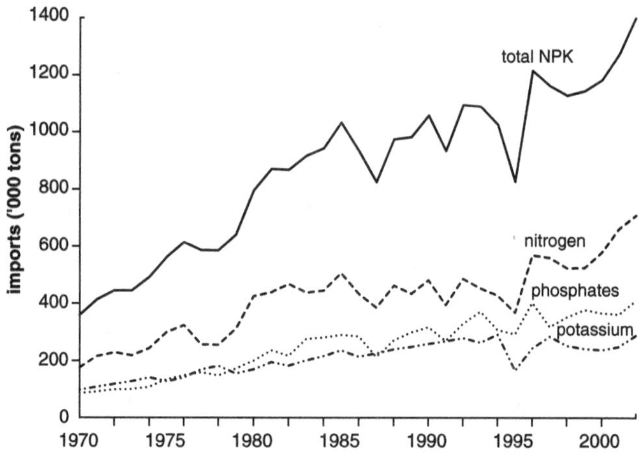

Source: FAOSTAT.

Strengthening Port Infrastructure. For many African countries, the scope
for negotiating bulk purchases of fertilizer and arranging bulk shipments
is limited by the lack of port facilities capable of handling large volumes.
Worldwide, the most commonly used vessels for shipping fertilizer are
20,000–25,000 metric tons, but few African ports outside South Africa can
accommodate even these medium-size vessels (exceptions include Abidjan,
Beira, Dakar, Dar es Salaam, Djibouti, Douala, Lagos, and Mombasa).
Most fertilizer imported into Africa is shipped via 10,000-metric-ton vessels.
This limits the size of bulk orders, and it entails a shipping cost premium
of between 10 and 15 percent over medium-size vessels.

Expanding capacity in the main ports of entry to allow larger vessels to
discharge is one obvious avenue for reducing the landed cost of fertilizer.
In Africa's low-volume developing markets, fertilizer importers and fertilizer distributors tend to be more concerned with capturing short-term
trading profits than in making long-term investments in transfer, storage,
and bagging infrastructure. "Third-party" firms also have little incentive to
invest in specialized infrastructure. Improvements in bulk unloading facilities may require public investment or joint public-private partnerships.

Pooling Import Orders. Rarely do importers in Africa pool orders, either
within the same country or among several different countries, and rarely
do they arrange for joint handling, storage, and distribution. Nor have the
multinational corporations that produce and market fertilizer invested in

landed inventory or large-scale market infrastructure in Africa as they have in other regions. Consequently, economies of scale are forfeited that could help to reduce the landed cost of imported fertilizer.

Incentives for reducing costs through joint procurement (not only pooling orders but also jointly chartering vessels), joint investment, and regional market expansion must be developed. Governments should explore opportunities for various forms of public-private partnerships while at the same time introducing safeguards to protect consumers against the concentration of market power. Multicountry trading blocks such as Malawi-Mozambique-Zambia or Malawi-Mozambique-Tanzania could take advantage of common ports, rail networks, and road systems to consolidate import orders. This strategy might require some harmonization of fertilizer formulas and regulatory frameworks. Models based on selling market franchises to single-source providers of fertilizer import services might also be feasible, even if rarely tested, in Africa.

Transitioning to Local Production. In the 2002/03 cropping season, Africa produced about 177,000 metric tons of fertilizer out of 147.9 million metric tons produced worldwide. Africa's capacity to produce fertilizer is not only limited, but it is also declining (figure 6.3).

Fertilizer production is capital-intensive and characterized by substantial economies of scale. A modern ammonia/urea complex capable of producing 550,000 metric tons of urea per year costs more than US$350

Figure 6.3 Fertilizer Production, Sub-Saharan Africa, 1970–2002

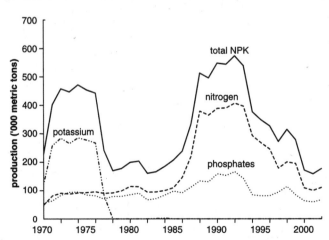

Source: FAOSTAT.

million to build. Factories producing other kinds of fertilizer—diammonium phosphate (DAP) and triple super phosphate (TSP)—must also be large to be competitive.

Few countries in Africa can justify the cost of investing in large, specialized plants. Not only do most African countries lack large domestic markets, but they also cannot count on reliable low-cost transportation links to world markets for exporting surplus production. Even more fundamental, only a handful of African countries have ready access to abundant supplies of the raw materials needed for fertilizer production: natural gas, phosphate rock, potassium salts, and sulfur. Angola, Mozambique, and Nigeria are among the countries in Africa that have some local fertilizer production potential. If the Southern Africa Development Community (SADC) countries lower trade barriers within the region, it might be possible, for example, to establish a profitable ammonia/urea production unit in Mozambique (using local natural gas) to supply the entire SADC market. Surplus production could be exported to countries in Asia.

Phasing Development of Facilities. Countries should be alert to changing opportunities for improving the cost-effectiveness of fertilizer sourcing, including a gradual transition to increased domestic processing of raw fertilizer materials. Figure 6.4 depicts how sourcing options can change as market size and capital costs change; the options extend from the importation of bagged products (less than 50,000 metric tons per year) to capital-intensive investments in developing indigenous resources (when demand for a single product exceeds 500,000 metric tons/year).

Several countries in Africa have invested in blending and bagging facilities, including Côte d'Ivoire, Malawi, Nigeria, Zambia, and Zimbabwe. Local blending offers four main advantages over importing preblended fertilizer. First, it can cost significantly less to purchase single-nutrient components in bulk. Second, compound fertilizers can be produced for crops in specific localities. Third, fertilizer packaging can be sized to meet local needs. Fourth, information on packages can be provided in local languages.

Reducing Distribution Costs

The farm-gate price of fertilizer is affected by transport, handling, and storage costs. In many African countries, investments in infrastructure offer large opportunities for reducing delivered prices of fertilizer.

Reducing Transport Costs. Whether fertilizer is imported or produced locally using imported ingredients, international shipping charges are an

Figure 6.4 Phased Development of Fertilizer Supply

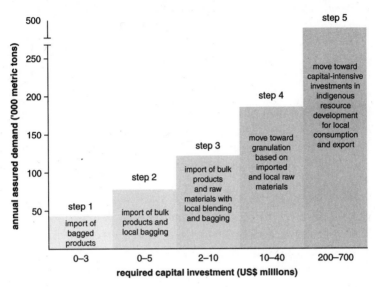

Source: Schultz and Parish 1989.

important cost component. Because virtually all fertilizer can be shipped in bulk at considerable freight savings over bagged cargo, consolidating orders for national or regional markets could increase lot sizes and reduce international shipping costs.

International shipping costs are frequently high, but they are often considerably lower than domestic transport costs. For example, a metric ton of fertilizer can be shipped 11,000 kilometers from a manufacturing plant in the United States to Mombasa, Kenya, for about US$50. To transport that metric ton of fertilizer less than 1,000 kilometers inland from Mombasa to Kampala, Uganda, would cost an additional US$80–US$90 per metric ton. To ship it another 300 kilometers to Mbarara, a Ugandan provincial capital, would cost another US$30–US$35 per metric ton. The cost of shipping the ton of fertilizer from Mombasa to Mbarara is thus about 2.5 times the cost of shipping it from the U.S. manufacturing plant to Mombasa.

Domestic transport costs are high in Africa because long distances must be covered and ground transport infrastructure is generally poor. Two main categories of domestic transport costs can be distinguished: (a) transport costs that are incurred in moving fertilizer from the import point to inland distribution centers and (b) transport costs that are incurred in moving fertilizer from inland distribution centers to the farm.

Fertilizer moves from import points to inland distribution centers via rail or road. Theoretically, rail transportation should be much cheaper than road transportation, but this is not always the case. Not only do railways in Africa—where they even exist—suffer frequent delays, but also covered wagons are not available, so fertilizer is exposed to rain, other harmful elements, and theft. Because shipping by rail is extremely risky, many fertilizer distributors in Africa rely on road transport, which is inherently more costly. Major road networks are often in poor condition. Transporters are subject to many official and unofficial tolls, taxes, and security checks, slowing delivery and imposing transaction costs. Because of interference, markets for surface transport services do not always operate competitively, and prices charged for transport services often include noneconomic rents.

Moving fertilizer to retailers and farmers is difficult because many rural areas in Africa are poorly served by feeder roads. Where feeder roads exist, they are often in poor condition and may be impassable for significant periods throughout the year. This poor infrastructure discourages fertilizer wholesalers from investing in their own retail market networks because they are reluctant to incur high transport costs in a situation where retail demand is weak and uncertain.

Reducing Handling Costs. Handling costs are commonly incurred for bagging bulk shipments, breaking standard 50-kilogram sacks into more appropriate sizes for smallholders, and loading and unloading sacks for multistage inland transport. The ability to reduce handling costs depends in part on the availability of equipment and facilities for bagging and blending. Dockside bagging with portable bagging equipment can be competitive with factory bagging, especially when local labor costs are low. In Africa, this is not always the case, and the additional costs incurred during local bagging sometimes exceed the cost savings achieved through bulk ocean freight rates. For example, a recent study showed that in 2003 the cost of dockside bagging in the port of Lagos, Nigeria, exceeded US$15 per metric ton (Gregory and Bumb 2006).

For many farmers, 50-kilogram bags are suitable, but for farmers cultivating small plots or facing credit constraints, smaller bags of 5, 10, or 25 kilograms may be more suitable. In a number of countries, including Malawi, Nigeria, and Zambia, retailers repackage fertilizer into smaller packs, for which they typically charge a premium of 14–15 percent. Although adding value for the retailers and improving convenience for small-scale farmers, this practice adds to already high retail prices.

Another handling cost is associated with frequent loading and unloading of fertilizer bags when inland shipments are broken up into numerous short-distance transactions. This cost typically occurs because of poor coordination along the supply chain. Although these handling costs usually are not a large share of retail prices, reducing the number of shipping/ storage steps between the port and the farmer can speed up delivery, reduce losses from frequent handling, and reduce costs. High transport costs often contribute to the problem of "stepwise delivery" by causing suppliers to maintain stocks in more accessible locations while supplying remote areas with multiple small shipments, rather than sending fewer large shipments that may not be completely sold and may have to be recovered at considerable expense.

Reducing Storage Costs. Storage costs are incurred in the short term (for example, when fertilizer is kept for a few days in a depot while being transported between locations) and also over the longer term (for example, when fertilizer is held for several months in a warehouse before the planting season). Short-term storage capacity is critical at import points, especially when fertilizer is imported by ship. Trucks are not always available to clear bulk shipments from the dock. Portside storage facilities reduce costly delays in offloading, regardless of whether the product is being bagged at the port. Long-term storage capacity is typically located at inland distribution centers, where large lots of fertilizer may need to be stored securely for extended periods at controlled moisture levels.

It is difficult to make a case that public funds should be used to support short-term fertilizer storage. Incentives are needed to stimulate commercial investment in short-term storage near port facilities, such as some type of public-private partnership or franchises to single-source providers. Long-term fertilizer storage, while generally unprofitable for the private fertilizer industry, arguably serves the public interest by improving the industry's capacity to respond quickly to unexpected changes in demand. If this is true, one potential response is to establish a national fertilizer reserve. The case for publicly supported strategic fertilizer reserves is similar to the case for publicly supported strategic grain reserves (World Bank 2006d). Strategic grain reserves have proven difficult to implement, however, and it is not clear that strategic fertilizer reserves would be any easier. In all likelihood, strategic fertilizer reserves would be just as costly to maintain.

Some of the problems encountered with strategic grain reserves could conceivably be overcome by setting up strategic fertilizer reserves along the following lines:

- Central bank–type autonomy, with complete independence from political processes and with clear, well-defined objectives
- Highly professional management, supported by a good information system and strong analytical capacity that includes demand forecasting skills
- Flexibility to hold the combination of fertilizer and financial reserves that minimizes costs within acceptable levels of risks
- Clear and open rules for market intervention, and transparency in interventions
- Access to a fund or financial markets to provide flexibility to respond in emergencies
- Use of insurance or hedging to reduce financial exposure

Strengthening Business Finance and Risk Management Instruments

Improving Business Finance. Fertilizer distribution in Africa, being dependent on importing, is extremely capital-intensive because (a) fertilizer purchases in international markets typically involve large volumes of product and outlays in the millions of dollars; (b) a year or more can elapse between the time when an advance payment is made to an overseas supplier and the time when proceeds are received from retail sales, and working capital must be financed during the entire interval; and (c) Africa's seasonal rainfall patterns require distributors to build up large inventories in advance of peak demand periods.

Most agricultural credit programs in Africa have attempted to address the credit needs of farmers. Relatively little attention has been paid to addressing the credit needs of input suppliers, including importers, wholesalers, and retailers. These three groups differ somewhat in their financial needs.

For fertilizer *importers*, financing issues typically revolve around the availability of foreign exchange and finding the collateral needed to obtain letters of credit for commercial loans. To date, few exporting countries are prepared to offer trade credits to support fertilizer sales to Africa, which is why donor assistance has been an important source of import credits.

Most fertilizer *wholesalers* in Africa have few fixed assets that they can pledge against repayment of working capital loans, and the prudential rules under which banks operate explicitly prohibit accepting fertilizer as surety for loans of working capital. In the absence of financial links with importers that can pass credit on to wholesalers, the latter are prevented from operating on a large scale and from reducing costs through economies of scale in transport and storage.

For fertilizer *retailers* (usually small businesses, located at the end of the supply chain where unit costs of the product are greatest), the major challenges involve not only improving access to credit but also developing the capacity to manage credit properly. Most retailers lack access to formal bank credit and lack the knowledge to engage successfully with formal financial institutions. As a result, they must rely on their own equity and retained earnings to finance new stocks, unless they can establish working relationships with suppliers that are willing to pass credit through to them. This substantially retards the rapid development of fertilizer retail markets, which in turn limits the size of wholesale markets.

By strengthening supply chains to enable the use of affordable trade credits, problems at all levels of the supply chain could be addressed. When supply chains are sufficiently transparent and the relationships among supply chain participants sufficiently strong, the participant with the strongest balance sheet can provide the necessary assurances to commercial banks for securing working capital loans. Once external financing is secured, it can be advanced to other supply chain participants in the form of trade credits. Normally the exporter is the participant with the strongest balance sheet. Exporter-provided financing is the main financial instrument for low-risk fertilizer distribution worldwide, but to date, there are few examples of exporter-provided financing in Africa (and where it does exist, it is rarely passed along the supply chain).

Business credit could be improved in other ways as well. Fertilizer importers could be encouraged to pool their financial resources, with the goal of building creditworthiness and jointly qualifying for export trade credits. Fertilizer stocks could be collateralized by establishing and regulating third-party-managed fertilizer distribution centers, so that inventories could be collateralized and easily liquidated by commercial banks in case of default. The development of secondary markets for fertilizer (box 6.1) would also reduce the risk of securing commercial bank loans with fertilizer inventories.

Governments can support these and other strategies by developing regulatory and legal frameworks that facilitate innovative financing mechanisms. Current links between the local financial sector and the fertilizer sector are so weak that the fertilizer sector is effectively constrained from developing. Financial sector experts should make it a priority to design and test fertilizer-backed securities and loan instruments.

Facilitating Risk Management. Fertilizer distributors in Africa face a number of significant risks:

- *Inventory risk.* Because effective demand for fertilizer can vary tremendously from year to year, fertilizer distributors often overstock, and in the absence of a secondary market for fertilizer, they must carry costly inventory from one season into the next.
- *Financing risk.* Most fertilizer retailers and even many wholesalers are unable to secure commercial credit to finance working inventory, so they rely on their own suppliers to provide inventory on credit. Those who extend fertilizer on credit—mainly importers and larger wholesalers—assume the risk of extending credit down the chain to trading partners and then not being repaid.
- *Price risk.* In Africa's highly volatile fertilizer markets, distributors who find themselves with unsold inventory sometimes liquidate their positions by dramatically discounting selling prices, with adverse consequences for other distributors.
- *Policy risk.* Policies relating to fertilizer in Africa have been notoriously inconsistent. Abrupt policy reversals have on a number of occasions caused sudden large changes in fertilizer availability and prices. Development organizations have sometimes promoted free or low-cost distribution of fertilizer.

Financial instruments for managing risks associated with fertilizer supply are generally lacking in Africa. With a few notable exceptions, such as South Africa, no third-party insurance can be purchased to cover inventory risk, financing risk, price risk, or policy risk. Some highly specialized risk-management instruments are currently being designed for piloting in a handful of countries.

Improving Supply-Chain Coordination Mechanisms

The term "supply chain" refers to a form of industrial organization in which one participant in a series of value-adding activities manages the assets of other participants or influences the activities carried out by other participants. Supply chains can be thought of as organizational pipelines for flows of (a) products and services; (b) payments, usually in the form of cash or

Box 6.1

Secondary Markets for Fertilizer

Secondary markets are markets for surplus goods. In secondary markets, surplus goods are transferred from sellers that cannot sell them immediately and wish to dispose of them to buyers who are prepared to purchase them for future sale. One reason why fertilizer distribution in Africa is so risky is that there are no formal secondary markets for fertilizer where distributors can dispose of excess inventory. Unless they can sell to another local dealer, fertilizer distributors must hold unsold stocks until the following planting season, which implies considerable financing costs and risks of spoilage. To avoid these problems, many fertilizer distributors in Africa consistently understock.

The development of secondary markets for fertilizer in Africa will require the creation of asset-backed security interests. Asset-backed securities are the contractual equivalent of physical inventory. They may be held by a third-party asset manager on behalf of the owner of the security. Asset managers are typically licensed, and as a condition of their license, they are required to comply with a set of professional standards and to purchase liability insurance for the benefit of the owners whose assets they manage. Commercial banks must be engaged in the process if the securities that are created are to become bankable and if they are to be accepted as collateral.

Trading fertilizer securities is much more efficient than trading physical stocks of fertilizer. In the absence of securities, fertilizer sales must be conducted on a quid pro quo barter basis without third-party intermediation or transacted as cash-based spot sales. Barter transactions and spot sales carry significant costs, because buyers as well as sellers must be present at the place of transfer, buyers as well as sellers must negotiate storage facilities to hold their stocks once ownership has been transferred, and the size of the sale is limited by the mode of conveyance that the buyer can secure immediately.

Secondary markets for fertilizer could be created in Africa by licensing brokers to buy surplus fertilizer inventories, which they could sell immediately into fertilizer-deficit areas or store for sale during a subsequent planting season. With some technical assistance, these brokered transactions could be expanded and formalized. For example, with the help of financial specialists, it should be possible to develop standard security contracts that are transferable electronically through designated exchanges.

trade credits; and (c) information, particularly information concerning the balance of demand and supply at the point of retail sale.

When a supply chain is functioning well, costs that individual participants would normally consider external are internalized, giving supply chain participants an incentive to work together to achieve mutually beneficial cost savings. The benefits that can be realized when supply chain participants coordinate their activities include lower-cost product sourcing; more efficient inventory management; better preservation of product integrity; improved trade financing; savings on transport, handling, storage, and bagging operations; prevention of physical losses; and increased investment in market development activities. Earlier discussions relating to fertilizer sourcing costs, physical distribution costs, and business finance and risk management instruments have repeatedly mentioned two broad strategies for reducing costs: expanding the market to allow economies of scale and improving coordination to remove process redundancies and inefficiencies. Both strategies can be effectively pursued through cooperative efforts between buyers and sellers that serve to integrate the supply chain.

Role of Government

Government has four major roles to play in promoting fertilizer supply chain development. These include introducing appropriate regulations, supporting market information systems, strengthening human capital, and building professional associations.

Introducing Appropriate Regulations

In industries characterized by significant economies of scale, including the fertilizer industry, government regulation is often required to ensure the emergence of supply chains that are not only strong and vibrant but also competitive. Regulation is particularly relevant in the many African countries that lack effective mechanisms for curbing market excesses that may result from weak and ineffective institutions (Gisselquist and Van der Meer 2001).

Direct government intervention in fertilizer markets through price controls or state-owned distribution systems is one approach to market regulation. Because past efforts of this nature in Africa have been costly and unsustainable, many governments are shifting from direct to indirect regulation of the fertilizer industry, which involves setting up rules and creating incentives to guide private actions and encourage investment.

One important regulatory function is to ensure that fertilizer importers and wholesalers refrain from collusive practices, including price fixing and market segmentation. Rules to ensure acceptable competitive practices must be developed, promulgated, and enforced through penalties. Unacceptable, anticompetitive conduct should be defined clearly, leaving little judicial ambiguity about what is legal and what is not. Technical assistance can be offered to develop laws, and enforcement mechanisms to realize these results.

Well-designed and properly enforced regulations can play a critical role in opening fertilizer markets. Markets can be opened by lowering trade barriers, integrating market information systems across national boarders, facilitating transnational mergers among national fertilizer companies, and creating market institutions that integrate multiple national markets.

Efforts to encourage competition in fertilizer markets should be tempered by the realization that in certain cases, excessive competition can frustrate the development of sustainable private sector–led markets (box 6.2). In these cases, it may be desirable temporarily to tolerate what might otherwise be considered a lack of competition to provide an opportunity for emerging fertilizer distribution firms to become established.

Another important regulatory function relates to quality control. Regulations relating to the chemical composition of fertilizer are often critically important to deter product adulteration, which can easily happen when fertilizer is repackaged. This is a perennial problem in Africa, where complaints about substandard fertilizer products are legion. Thus, it may be appropriate to introduce regulations establishing clearly defined assay standards for a standardized and limited set of fertilizers, as well as penalties for distributors whose products do not conform to those standards. Because regulations are meaningless if they cannot be enforced, the introduction of product quality controls will often need to be accompanied by supporting investments in facilities for carrying out rapid, low-cost testing.

Sometimes the problem is not that fertilizer products have been adulterated but that buyers are given inaccurate information about proper application methods, exaggerated descriptions of the expected benefits, or both. Therefore, regulations may also be needed to govern the implementation and enforcement of standards for retail packaging with regard to claims about a product's "effectiveness" and "best application."

Box 6.2

Can Too Much Competition in Fertilizer Markets Be Undesirable?

During the period when an emerging fertilizer sector is weakly capitalized and actors are still learning efficient procurement and logistics management methods, intense competition among a large number of inexperienced actors may result in undesirable outcomes. In pursuit of short-term profits, firms may be tempted to engage in opportunistic behavior, dipping in and out of the market to take advantage of temporary cross-border trade opportunities presented by short-term exchange rate fluctuations, or taking advantage of below-cost fertilizer supplies available through periodic auctions of donor-supplied fertilizer aid. When not supported by investments needed to establish the basis for a long-term presence in the market, opportunistic behavior of this nature in pursuit of temporary profit can be detrimental to the long-term development of sustainable, low-cost supply networks.

Faced with this kind of "destructive" competition, policy makers may decide that it is desirable to accept a certain amount of industrial concentration, especially during the early stages of market development, if that industrial concentration can help achieve economies of scale and contribute to more reliable fertilizer supplies. For example, they may consider temporarily promoting "competition *for* the fertilizer market" instead of "competition *in* the fertilizer market." Under a policy of "competition *for* the market," qualified importers and distributors are granted exclusive rights for a specified period in exchange for a commitment to expand fertilizer markets and develop geographically extensive distribution networks. Those granted exclusive rights would typically be required to contribute toward the cost of strengthening market infrastructure (including port facilities, blending and packaging facilities, and storage facilities).

Because industrial concentration brings with it the risk of undesirable monopoly power, the behavior of participating firms must be monitored carefully, and regulatory authorities must be prepared to step in and discourage abuses. It is extremely important in such cases that (a) the terms of these concession or market franchise agreements are developed in a manner that protects the public from the excesses of monopolistic behavior and that (b) governments have the legal institutions and judicial capacity to enforce the terms of the agreements.

Supporting Market Information Systems

Fertilizer sellers need information to decide how much product to procure to meet projected demand. On one hand, if sellers are unable to match supply and demand, either they forfeit earnings because of stock shortages, or they incur costs associated with holding unsold inventory. Fertilizer buyers, on the other hand, need information about the inventory levels being retained by sellers, as well as information about current and expected future prices. If buyers are unable to make informed judgments about when and where to purchase fertilizer, they may be unable to acquire sufficient quantities, or they may end up paying unnecessarily high prices.

Private firms have few incentives to provide market information services, because if they invest in collecting, compiling, and distributing market information, they cannot easily prevent buyers of their services from reselling the information to others. A strong case can therefore be made for public investment in collection and distribution of market information. Many countries in Africa do have public market information systems, but these systems tend to focus mainly on farm outputs, and the mechanisms for disseminating market information are weak. Even so, these systems can serve as models and perhaps even platforms for expanding the collection, analysis, and dissemination of information on input markets.

Over the longer term, public-private partnerships could be explored to support the development of market information systems that would not only monitor and report fertilizer prices but also report inventory levels and market trends. Government statistical agencies could develop tenders for franchised market information services that could be offered to qualified investors. Some of the information collected by franchise holders would be made publicly available, and some would be sold on a commercial basis to interested users.

Strengthening Human Capital

A third area in which government can help to strengthen fertilizer supply chains in Africa relates to strengthening human capital. Many fertilizer wholesalers and retailers have some formal training in a technical field related to agriculture, but few have undergone formal business training, partly because few formal training programs exist in Africa for retailers, warehousemen, wholesale distributors, or importers.

The lack of formal training opportunities is problematic, because business skills matter a great deal in the development of efficient distribution channels. Rural agrodealer support programs pioneered in Kenya and Malawi by the Rockefeller Foundation demonstrate this. The programs have trained hundreds of retailers in efficient business practice, finance, and working capital management. They have helped dealers secure trade credits, some of which have been passed on to customers, and they have promoted the development of commercial networks within which inventory risk can be limited. Among other things, these programs have demonstrated that the most effective way to deliver increased quantities of fertilizer to farmers is to combine a supply-push strategy with a demand-pull strategy that promotes supplier-financed demonstration plots and product training for retailers. The key to success, moreover, lies in ensuring a smooth interface between supply and demand at the end of the supply chain where retailers and farmers interact. In many ways, retailers are the key link. Not only do they understand the needs, constraints, and ability to pay of farmers within their market territories, but also they are well placed to help manage many of the supply-side risks.

Building Professional Associations

Many of the firms that distribute fertilizer in Africa invest in a range of businesses. Depending on their assessment of risks and returns, they focus their efforts on activities that offer the best risk-adjusted returns. Often these are not fertilizer-related. Variable demand, high costs, low profit margins, and a significant level of risk discourage investment in fertilizer distribution and provide limited incentives for new product development. One potential remedy to this problem is to foster the development of professional associations that can serve as focal points for self-help programs and provide networked access to other similarly constituted professional groups in other countries. By working with local educational institutions, they can develop a professional training curriculum and a professional certification process. Finally, they can facilitate the self-regulation of members with respect to ethical dealing and compliance with procompetitiveness laws.

CHAPTER 7

Rethinking the Role of Fertilizer Subsidies

Need for a Long-Term Perspective on Public Interventions

In considering possible entry points for public interventions to increase fertilizer use in Africa, it is important to adopt a long-term perspective. Past efforts to promote fertilizer in Africa often have focused narrowly on stimulating immediate increases in fertilizer use with the help of fertilizer price subsidies—budgetary payments made by governments or development partners to reduce the cost of fertilizer at the farm level. This approach is very limited, however, because governments can do many things to promote fertilizer beyond artificially reducing the price. Public interventions can be used to help not only farmers but also traders, financial services providers, and other key actors on the supply side. More fundamentally, public interventions can involve not only direct budgetary payments designed to influence fertilizer prices in the short run but also a wide range of other measures that improve the profitability of fertilizer over the medium to long run by directly or indirectly influencing market prices, costs incurred, or benefits received by consumers and producers of fertilizer.

Policy makers and development partners must work to identify and implement interventions aimed at addressing the underlying structural problems that undermine incentives for farmers to use fertilizer and for firms to supply fertilizer. Previous sections of this report have described a large number of good practice interventions that can be used to strengthen demand for fertilizer, supply of fertilizer, or both. Many of these interventions are designed to attack the underlying structural constraints that combine to undermine the profitability of fertilizer use. Although all of them can potentially contribute to increased use of fertilizer in Africa, none is likely to be effective if implemented in isolation. Policy makers and development partners who are seeking to bring about more sustainable increases in fertilizer use must select combinations of these measures to ensure that demand and supply can grow in parallel, thus providing the basis for the emergence of viable private sector–led commercial fertilizer markets. The optimal combination will likely differ depending on the stage of development in which the fertilizer market finds itself.

Rethinking the Role of Fertilizer Subsidies

Where does this leave fertilizer subsidies? In the past, fertilizer promotion programs in Africa relied heavily on the use of fertilizer price subsidies. As discussed in chapter 3, various economic arguments can be made to justify the use of fertilizer price subsidies. Although many of these arguments are valid in principle, in practice the experience in Africa with fertilizer price subsidies has not been good. Whenever fertilizer price subsidies have been used, the results have generally been disappointing: the cost of the subsidies has often been high, and the benefits generated by the incremental fertilizer use have usually been modest.

Despite their history of disappointing results, fertilizer subsidies are now attracting renewed attention in Africa. Recently, there has been considerable debate about the desirability of using fertilizer subsidies to achieve not only economic growth targets but also welfare goals. Although it is difficult to support the use of fertilizer subsidies on efficiency grounds, realistically it must be recognized that fertilizer subsidies are likely to be implemented in some African countries, if for no other reason than their political popularity. The political appeal of fertilizer subsidies is understandable. For politicians, fertilizer subsidies can be used to pursue important policy goals, such as increasing agricultural productivity, improving food security, and reducing poverty and hunger. At the same time, fertilizer subsidies also provide a convenient instrument for channeling income support to large numbers of constituents, many of whom may be very poor and deserving of public assistance.

Appealing though they may be, however, fertilizer subsidies should be viewed with extreme caution. With the weight of empirical evidence now showing that fertilizer subsidies are likely to be inefficient, costly, and fiscally unsustainable, policy makers seeking strategies to promote increased fertilizer use would be well advised to adopt a broad view encompassing a range of possible support options. In selecting among these support options, they should consider the potential benefits and costs of alternative uses of scarce public expenditures.

The bottom line adopted by this report with regard to subsidies is simple and straightforward: *if subsidies are to be used to promote fertilizer use, they should be market-smart.* The rest of this chapter describes a number of market-smart subsidies—innovative ways of using public resources to promote fertilizer that have been piloted with varying degrees of success in Africa and elsewhere.

Design and Implementation of Market-Smart Subsidies

Market-smart subsidies are temporary interventions that work singly or in combination to lower the price and/or improve the availability of fertilizer at the farm level in ways that encourage efficient use of fertilizer while at the same time promoting private investment in fertilizer markets. The main differences between traditional fertilizer subsidies and market-smart fertilizer subsidies are that market-smart fertilizer subsidies are temporary, they do not distort the relative price of fertilizer relative to other inputs so as to encourage excessive and economically inefficient use of fertilizer, and they are designed to shift incentives faced by buyers and sellers in ways that are consistent with the development of sustainable private markets for fertilizer. Market-smart subsidies also differ from traditional subsidies in that they target a wider range of potential entry points, not just the price paid by farmers when they purchase fertilizer.

In designing interventions to promote increased fertilizer use, policy makers and project designers should bear in mind the following 10 guiding principles if they want subsidies to be market-smart:

1. *Promote fertilizer as part of a wider strategy.* Fertilizer is not a magic bullet. Interventions designed to promote increased use of fertilizer should be developed within the context of a wider sector strategy that recognizes the importance of supplying comple- mentary inputs, strengthening output markets, and appropriately sequencing interventions.

2. *Favor market-based solutions.* Long-term solutions to the fertilizer problem will have to be market-based. Interventions designed to promote increased use of fertilizer should be designed to support market development and not undermine incentives for private sector investment.

3. *Promote competition.* Competition in fertilizer markets is needed to ensure good performance. Barriers to entry into fertilizer distribution should be reduced (except possibly in the very short run), and markets should be competitive to ensure the lowest-cost and best-quality service.

4. *Pay attention to demand.* Farmers' effective demand, shaped by the current or potential profitability of fertilizer use, should be the ultimate driving force of input supply systems and the foundation of a sustainable fertilizer promotion strategy.

5. *Insist on economic efficiency.* Fertilizer promotion efforts should be driven by economic considerations. Interventions designed to promote increased use of fertilizer should be carried out only where fertilizer use is economically efficient.

6. *Empower farmers.* Farmers should be in the driver's seat. Interventions designed to promote increased use of fertilizer should empower farmers to make their own decisions on the most appropriate way to manage soil fertility in their particular farming context.

7. *Devise an exit strategy.* Governments should not be in the fertilizer distribution business for the long haul. Public sector interventions designed to promote increased use of fertilizer should be designed with a clear exit strategy, except for a few long-run public-good functions such as market regulation, infrastructural development, and research and development on natural resources management.

8. *Pursue regional integration.* Market size matters, so trade matters. Countries should seek regional integration and harmonization of fertilizer policies to reap economies of size and scope, which are especially important in a region such as Africa with so many small countries.

9. *Ensure sustainability.* Solutions must be designed for the long term. Interventions designed to promote increased use of fertilizer should be economically, institutionally, and environmentally sustainable.

10. *Promote pro-poor growth.* Equity considerations matter. Assuming that the previous nine guiding principles have been followed, a final consideration is that public interventions designed to promote increased use of fertilizer should also aim to promote pro-poor growth. In exceptional circumstances, poverty reduction or food

security objectives may even be given precedence over efficiency and sustainability goals, if it can be determined that fertilizer interventions are a cost-effective way of addressing these problems.

When Market-Smart Subsidies Can Be Helpful

Most governments in Africa are interested in promoting increased fertilizer use because it can contribute to long-term improvements in agricultural productivity and sometimes to conservation of natural resources. In this context, the main policy objective is often to stimulate the development of an efficient and profitable fertilizer marketing system that will contribute to agricultural productivity growth. Achievement of this policy objective can often be supported by market-smart subsidies targeted at the following entry points:

- *Promoting technology adoption and fostering farmer learning.* By providing incentives directly to farmers, market-smart subsidies can be used to encourage farmers to test fertilizer and other improved technologies that they otherwise would have avoided as too risky.
- *Improving the supply chain for productivity-increasing agricultural inputs.* By strengthening input supply chains, market-smart subsidies can increase the availability of improved inputs at affordable prices, thereby increasing the profitability of fertilizer use.
- *Capturing economies of scale in nascent fertilizer industries.* By increasing aggregate demand for fertilizer and providing incentives to retailers, wholesalers, importers, and others, market-smart subsidies can allow the domestic fertilizer industry to capture economies of scale in sourcing, packaging, storing, marketing, and sometimes even producing fertilizer.

Promoting Fertilizer Use to Raise Agricultural Productivity Growth

During the past decade, some innovative approaches have been piloted to stimulate increased fertilizer use as a way of promoting agricultural productivity growth. (Approaches for promoting increased fertilizer use as a safety net measure are discussed later in this chapter.) All of these approaches have shortcomings, but they provide examples of how public resources—subsidies—can be used to promote fertilizer use in ways that are more likely to foster the emergence of sustainable, private sector–led fertilizer markets than traditional approaches do, especially the indiscriminate distribution of low-cost or free fertilizer.

Demonstration Packs

Distribution of small packs of subsidized (even free) fertilizer, along with complementary inputs such as improved seed and relevant technical advice, can be a good way to introduce farmers to fertilizer and encourage experimentation and learning. Although the Malawi Starter Pack Program is perhaps the best-known example, demonstration pack programs have been implemented in many countries in Africa. Some of these programs clearly succeeded in getting new technology—including fertilizer—into the hands of farmers who otherwise would have been unlikely to take them up, and in this respect the demonstration pack programs were quite successful.

Demonstration pack programs are prone to potential problems, however, if they are not designed and implemented with care. The key to success lies in making sure that the demonstration packs end up only (or at least mostly) in the hands of farmers who are unfamiliar with fertilizer and would not have used fertilizer in the absence of the program. If the demonstration packs end up in the hands of farmers who already know about fertilizer and are likely to use the subsidized fertilizer in lieu of purchased fertilizer, then the main effect of the program will be to transfer income to farmers (via the subsidy) and displace commercial sales. Depending on the size of the subsidy, the incentives to acquire subsidized fertilizer can be quite high, which explains why many demonstration pack programs have been subject to elite capture, with much of the subsidized fertilizer ending up in the hands of relatively well-off farmers.

The success of demonstration pack programs thus is likely to depend on the effectiveness with which the fertilizer and associated inputs can be targeted effectively. By far the most commonly used method of targeting involves the use of vouchers (discussed below). Another method for targeting that has been tried less frequently, and with mixed success, includes physical distribution of seed, fertilizer, and other inputs to eligible farmers through centralized distribution points (for example, government storage centers).

Vouchers

Input vouchers are a market-smart form of subsidy that permit voucher holders to purchase specific quantities and types of farm inputs from qualified distributors who have agreed to accept vouchers as payment.

The distributors in turn redeem the vouchers for cash payment from the program organizers.

Voucher programs normally include (a) a mechanism for selecting voucher recipients and for distributing the vouchers to these recipients, (b) a system for financing the distribution of inputs and for moving them through supply chains to qualified distributors, and (c) a mechanism for managing the cash redemption of vouchers accepted by distributors. Typically, voucher programs rely on existing commercial supply chains and involve rural financial institutions that are willing to serve as agents for the distribution and redemption of vouchers.

Vouchers can be used to augment the power of farmers to purchase fertilizer, either by reducing the price of fertilizer (if the voucher is given to the farmer for free or sold below market cost) or by providing farmers with additional liquidity (if the voucher serves as production credit, with repayment expected at some later date). Vouchers targeted at input distributors can be used to augment the purchasing power of input distributors in similar fashion.

The liquidity of vouchers varies depending on the rules established for their distribution, exchange, and redemption, which can vary considerably depending on the objectives of the voucher program and the ingenuity of those managing the program. Usually, vouchers are not quite equivalent to cash, because in most cases they are subject to rules established to meet specific program goals. For example, because vouchers typically are used as a way of targeting fertilizer subsidies, they are usually distributed to only certain groups in the population. Alternatively, they may be distributed through self-targeting mechanisms, as (for example) when they are given to those who have performed community labor. In an effort to reduce "leakage" (diversion of the subsidy to individuals who are not part of the target group), transfer of vouchers to a person other than the original recipient may be prohibited. Alternatively, redemption by a person other than the designated recipient may be allowed, but to discourage transfers, redemption may be allowed only at a lower redemption value.

Use of vouchers as part of a demand-pull strategy to promote increased fertilizer use has several potential advantages:

- Vouchers can build additional demand for fertilizer and thus accelerate fertilizer market development if the targeted farmers are not already using fertilizer.
- Voucher programs can be designed to run for a number of years, during which time fertilizer subsidies are gradually removed (for example, by

reducing the value of the vouchers as a share of input costs) so that farmers and distributors can make the transition to an economically sustainable cash market.

- Vouchers can be used to target specific groups of farmers (producers of certain crops, producers located in specific regions or production environments, or producers who fall into a particular social stratum or income class).

Use of voucher programs also has some potential disadvantages:

- Voucher programs can be costly to design and implement, particularly if subsidies are involved that entail measures to control corruption and rent seeking.
- Voucher programs can fail to achieve their objectives if convertible vouchers are purchased by intermediaries and a secondary market emerges for their resale and use. In such cases, direct cash transfers could be more effective.

Matching Grants

Matching grants are another type of market-smart subsidy that can be used to fund start-up activities. Under the typical matching grant program, the recipient of the matching grant (which can be an individual, a group of individuals, a firm, or a not-for-profit organization) is required to mobilize local resources, which are then combined with external funding (the matching grant) to pursue a defined set of objectives. Because a matching grant is usually provided on a one-off basis to a given recipient, it does not imply a recurring commitment of resources on the part of the granting agency, meaning that it is usually easy to devise an exit strategy. Most matching grant programs simply terminate as soon as the initial allocation of funds has been fully disbursed. Matching grants can be particularly useful in situations where credit markets are weak, financial risk is high, or both. In such cases, the public or donor funds are used to leverage private investments until financial and risk markets emerge.

Matching grants can be used to promote fertilizer market development at three levels in the supply chain by fostering agricultural innovation, business development, and community-driven investment:

- *Agricultural innovation grants* can be awarded—usually through competitive procedures—directly to producer organizations or to partnerships of farmers and research and extension services to develop and test innovations related to soil fertility and other types of innovations, depending on farmers' priorities. Farmers' involvement ensures that local demand increasingly guides the development and dissemination of technology. The approach shows promise, but it requires substantial local public and private financial support and a highly professional unit to administer the program. Grants may be managed completely by farmer groups to allow them to test and adapt new technologies, as is being implemented for soil fertility management and complementary practices in Tanzania (box 7.1).

- *Business development grants* can be awarded competitively to individual entrepreneurs or to entire firms. These grants are generally designed to improve business performance by encouraging investment in business processes or staff capacity building. In the fertilizer sector, they can be used to encourage risk taking (for example, by stipulating that recipients must expand fertilizer distribution into new market areas or carry new product lines).
- *Community-driven development grants* can be used to support agricultural income generation at the community level. Direct transfers for productive activities, including investment in soil fertility, may be justified if they reduce poverty by targeting the very poor and if they stimulate some private sector development. By encouraging recipients to engage in collective action to obtain technical support, purchase inputs, or market outputs, community-driven development grants can provide options that are not open to individuals acting alone.

Matching grants have some drawbacks, however. Administration of matching grant programs can be costly, because it is often difficult to distinguish between needy applicants who really are unable to mobilize investment resources on their own and more well-off applicants who are perfectly capable of accessing commercial credit. If this distinction is not maintained, matching grants can end up going to creditworthy recipients, thereby crowding out private sector lending. Finally, matching grant programs are ripe for political manipulation, and administrators of matching grant programs often come under pressure to steer grants to those with political and economic influence.

Because matching grants are generally market-smart, they have been growing in popularity. Still, considerable care is needed in designing a matching grant program (McKean and Ostrom 1995; Van der Meer and

Box 7.1

Agricultural Innovation Grants Empower Farmers in Tanzania

In Tanzania, the Participatory Agricultural Development and Empowerment Project (PADEP) is seeking to raise the production of food, incomes, and assets of participating households in about 840 villages by implementing small agricultural development subprojects planned and managed by community members and farmers' groups. Participants learn how to select appropriate technologies and matching grants, which are provided for a fixed period to allow them to purchase the necessary inputs, including fertilizers.

The project uses a matching grant mechanism to offset the risk of technology adoption. The approach is to share 50 percent of the cost of technology adoption up to approximately US$25 equivalent per household for two farming seasons, rather than subsidize a single input. Rural communities and farmers' groups select profitable technologies, and the matching grant makes fertilizer, seeds, seedlings, plant protection agents, implements, and any other needed inputs affordable during the period of adoption (in most cases, for a duration of two years). Inputs are purchased from the private sector. In addition, the project will contribute 100 percent of the cost of technical assistance and training, up to a maximum of US$3,000 per village.

A second component of the project addresses deficiencies in marketing of farm inputs, particularly improved seeds, fertilizers, and pesticides, through (for example) promotion of dealers' associations. A training program has been initiated for retailers and other local input traders on effective handling of agricultural inputs, setting up demonstration plots for these inputs at the village and district levels, and providing reliable technical information.

Noordam 2004). Experience suggests that grant programs are much more likely to be successful when some simple guidelines are followed:

- The type of grant selected should be tailored to local circumstances, including the quality of local technical expertise.
- The economic rationale for public cofinancing should be articulated clearly.
- Rigorous and transparent eligibility criteria and assessment procedures are important, as is competent fund management with clear objectives and procedures.

- To ensure that proposals address private sector priorities, an initial investment may be desirable to build the capacity of potential recipients so that they can develop and defend proposals that identify key problems, critically evaluate alternative solutions, and justify grant funding based on clear net benefits in economic and social terms.
- A significant learning period should be allowed to enable stakeholders to gain experience in working with the grant scheme and to make adjustments as necessary.
- Administrative costs must be controlled rigorously to create a sustainable private market for support services within a limited period. Fifteen percent appears to be an international norm for start-up and staffing costs, administering grants, monitoring and evaluation, institutional development, and training to prepare proposals.
- Often there are trade-offs between ensuring that operations are cost-effective and ensuring that they are conducted with accountability and transparency, and some balance must be sought so that both objectives are met.
- Grant funding is typically most effective when it is complemented by other funding mechanisms. In many cases, block funding from the public sector will still be needed to address core public goods.
- From the beginning, grant schemes should have a clear disengagement strategy. Proposals should include action steps that can be monitored, with milestones and targets indicating when objectives have been achieved. Generally, grants should be for a fixed period (for example, three years) and nonrenewable.

Loan Guarantees

Risk is often an important constraint affecting both the demand and supply side of fertilizer markets and is especially constraining for the development of sustainable markets to finance fertilizer purchases, whether by farmers or by traders. A number of promising approaches have been used to reduce risks to private lenders. One relatively simple approach is to partially guarantee loans to farmers or input dealers for a defined period. A 50 percent guarantee is usually sufficient to motivate lenders to finance input purchases, but at the same time it provides incentives to lenders to carefully scrutinize loans so that the guarantor—usually the government or a development partner—incurs only a negligible financial burden. The level of guarantee should not be set too high (for example, the 100 percent guarantee used in Ethiopia provides no incentive to lenders to evaluate the creditworthiness of a borrower), and it should be phased out over time as lender and borrower develop a trustful relationship. Guaranteed loans underwritten by the Rockefeller Foundation have been used successfully to promote the development of input dealer networks in Kenya, Malawi, and Uganda. (box 7.2).

Box 7.2

Developing Agricultural Input Supply Systems in Kenya, Malawi, and Uganda

The Rockefeller Foundation is supporting three organizations to develop agricultural input supply pipelines in rural Kenya, Malawi, and Uganda, with an emphasis on three key factors: affordability, accessibility, and incentives. The project features four activities:

- Training of input retailers to develop their technical, product, and business management skills. After they have completed the training, retailers are certified as "agrodealers."
- Certified agrodealers may qualify to be linked via credit guarantees to major agricultural input supply firms, which supply them with stocks for a 30–60 day credit period. The credit guarantee covers 50 percent of the risk of default.
- To improve affordability of inputs for farmers, the agrodealers pack and sell seeds and fertilizers in small packages, ranging from a 1-kilogram pack for seeds to between 2-kilogram and 10-kilogram packs for fertilizers.
- To help achieve economies of scale in sourcing and transporting fertilizers and other inputs, some agrodealers have formed purchasing groups at the district level—with group members providing joint collateral to guarantee the supply of inputs from the companies. Furthermore, the agrodealers have organized themselves into national-level agrodealer associations that allow them to better negotiate for lower prices and better credit financing arrangements with the agricultural input supply companies and to influence government policy.

As the numbers of agrodealers have expanded, the flow of farm inputs, particularly fertilizers and improved seeds, into rural areas has increased significantly. For example, a recent survey of rural markets in Malawi showed that the majority of farmers in areas covered by the program now buy their inputs from a network of 322 certified agrodealers, compared with buying directly from the government parastatal. The distances that the poor travel in search of inputs have been drastically reduced in many districts as the number of agrodealers expanded. The sale of fertilizers by certified rural dealers rose from US$125,000 at the end of April 2003 to US$676,000 at the end of April 2004. The default rate on the credit guarantee over the past three years has been less than 1 percent. Finally, the agrodealers have also become important extension nodes for the rural poor.

Promoting Fertilizer Use as a Safety Net for the Poor

Separate from the arguments made in favor of using fertilizer subsidies as a way of stimulating increased agricultural productivity growth is the argument that fertilizer subsidies can be used as an instrument for achieving welfare goals. The latter can be made in two ways: (1) fertilizer subsidies can be used on a long-term basis to provide income support to the chronic poor, and (2) fertilizer subsidies can be used on a short-term basis to help the temporarily poor recover more quickly from acute income shortfalls, especially following a natural disaster such as a drought.

These arguments for using fertilizer subsidies to provide a safety net for the poor are grounded in the insight that fertilizer subsidies can provide a less costly way to ensure food security at the household level than alternative approaches (such as importing food commercially or distributing food aid). The authors of the UN Millennium Project (2005) report argue that providing "fertilizer aid" is more cost-effective than providing food aid, because a given expenditure on fertilizer produces more food in the location in which it is needed than would the same expenditure when used to support traditional food aid relief programs.

Theoretically speaking, the argument in favor of fertilizer aid is valid, as long as certain relationships hold between the cost of providing fertilizer and the cost of providing food aid. More generally, proponents of fertilizer aid raise a useful point about the value of basing policy and program decisions on the relative costs of alternative interventions. At the same time, it is important to recognize that the economic case for fertilizer aid rests on a number of key assumptions, including some that are unlikely to hold in the real world, at least not all of the time. The most debatable of these include the following: (a) fertilizer subsidies can be targeted effectively to food-deficient households, (b) growing conditions will necessarily allow farmers to achieve yield levels needed for the fertilizer investment to "multiply" into the total amount of food needed, and (c) the only policy alternative to providing fertilizer aid is to provide food aid.

The appropriateness of fertilizer aid and how it might be provided depend in part on how well food and fertilizer markets are functioning. Table 7.1 depicts options that could be considered in a simple dichotomous world of well-functioning and poorly functioning food and fertilizer markets:

The upper-left quadrant in table 7.1 represents situations, usually associated with remote regions, in which neither food nor fertilizer markets are working well. In such cases, distributing both food (especially for emergencies) and possibly fertilizer might be justified as safety nets. Even though input markets may function poorly, it still should be possible to use such programs to help build private sector capacity (for example, by contracting fertilizer delivery to private suppliers or providing technical assistance to input retailers).

The lower-right quadrant in the table represents situations in which both food and fertilizer markets are functioning reasonably well. In such cases, the trend in safety net programs is now to provide cash transfers, instead of food aid, so as to give households maximum flexibility and to reinforce development of local food production and markets. There is

Table 7.1 Use of Fertilizer Aid Programs in Different Market Situations

	Fertilizer markets	
Food markets	Function poorly	Function well
Function poorly	SR: Food aid and (possibly) fertilizer aid LR: Build household assets (may include soil fertility through market-smart subsidies) **combined with** measures to strengthen input and output markets	Not applicable in practice
Function well	SR: Cash transfers LR: Build household assets (may include soil fertility through market-smart subsidies) **combined with** measures to strengthen input markets	SR: Cash transfers LR: Build household assets (may include soil fertility through market-smart subsidies)

Source: Authors.
SR = short run, LR = long run.

Box 7.3

Starter Pack and Targeted Inputs Programs: Lessons Learned in Malawi

The Starter Pack Program and its successor, the Targeted Inputs Program (TIP), were implemented by the government of Malawi with financial assistance from numerous development partners, beginning in the 1998/99 cropping season. In its initial years of operation, the initiative provided almost every rural smallholder household with a free "pack" consisting of 15 kilograms of fertilizer, 2 kilograms of hybrid maize seed, and 1 kilogram of legume seed. The inputs were sufficient for cultivation of 0.1 hectare, according to extension recommendations (Oygard et al. 2003).

The Starter Pack Program was intended to meet several objectives: increasing maize yields and food security, countering soil nutrient depletion, and making a new line of fertilizer-responsive semiflint maize hybrids available to small farmers who otherwise might not take the risk to experiment with them. The Starter Pack Program was originally conceived as a technology-based plan that was cheaper than importing maize, but in later years it and its successor program (TIP) doubled as a relief effort. The program also had a strong political dimension because it was clearly intended to demonstrate the government's efforts to "do something" to help rural households (Levy 2005).

Pros. During the initial years when every household nationwide was a recipient, the Starter Pack Program succeeded in putting improved technology in the hands of many poor farmers who otherwise would not have been able to afford these inputs. Consequently, for the several years during which the program operated at this scale, rural households' food security and income position was improved (Cromwell et al. 2001; Levy and Barahona 2002; Oygard et al. 2003). Evaluation data showed that in the 1998/99 and 1999/2000 cropping seasons, starter packs raised maize production (on average) by about 125–150 kilograms per household, which was significantly more than was estimated in the project design. Although it is difficult to define the marginal contribution made by starter packs (because maize production in Malawi is greatly influenced by rainfall levels and other weather-related factors), total production of maize in each of those two years was approximately 500,000 metric tons higher than ever before or since and 67 percent higher than the 22-year average. Fertilizer importers liked the program because program fertilizer was purchased from established importers, rather than imported through independent channels.

(Continued)

Cons. The original Starter Pack Program was neither a safety net program nor a longer-term development program; rather, it was something in between—a stop-gap program, imposing high financial opportunity costs in terms of forgone investments in infrastructure, extension, and market development that could drive down the costs of input and output marketing and thus contribute to long-run fertilizer use (Levy and Barahona 2002). During the TIP phase, when the program was scaled down to reduce the financial burden borne by government and development partners, efforts to target relatively poor households proved ineffective, even though targeting the poorest of the poor was a key objective (Mann 2003). In addition, the robust and widely verified technologies that had formed the components of the original starter pack were changed, and the link with science and to economically viable improved technologies was lost.

Among the many lessons learned from the starter pack and TIP experiences, three stand out:

1. Distribution of subsidized inputs (including fertilizer) must be accompanied by robust and scientifically validated management recommendations.
2. Given political economy considerations, it is extremely difficult to target fertilizer subsidies effectively so they reach only the poorest of the poor.
3. Subsidized inputs (including fertilizer) can do little to improve food security in years when food crop production is severely affected by drought.

Source: Blackie 2006.

little reason to prefer fertilizer transfers unless they are seen as a form of forced savings (for example, they may be less subject to social obligations for immediate expenditure than cash) or unless holding cash may be more insecure because of risk of theft. Cash safety net transfers are best complemented by asset-building programs over the longer term to move households into a food-secure status. Fertilizer subsidies may be part of such longer-run programs, but they should follow the market-smart strategies discussed above (for example, matching grants and vouchers).

The lower-left quadrant in table 7.1 represents situations in which food markets work relatively well, but input markets are poorly developed. Here the strategy would be similar to that in the first case, but with additional efforts to build input markets.

The upper-right quadrant in the table represents situations in which fertilizer markets work relatively well, but food markets are

Box 7.4

Fertilizer Support Program: Lessons Learned in Zambia

In Zambia, fertilizer subsidies constitute the single largest expenditure item in the Ministry of Agriculture and Cooperatives (MACO) budget. During the 2005/06 cropping season, MACO's Fertilizer Support Programme (FSP) cost more than 140 billion Zambian kwacha, representing more than 40 percent of MACO spending—more than expenditure on staff salaries and operating costs combined. Taking into account agricultural programs funded through other ministries, the FSP share of total agricultural spending constituted 30 percent of outlays, and it remained by a large margin the largest expenditure item.

To what extent is the FSP achieving its objectives of increasing food production, alleviating rural poverty, and improving food security among rural households? The impacts of the FSP were assessed through a study using data from the 2002/03 cropping season. Noteworthy findings included:

- Eight percent of smallholder farmers reported receiving FSP fertilizer. This compares with 16 percent of smallholder farmers who reported buying fertilizer in the market. About one-third of all fertilizer used by smallholders reportedly came from the FSP.
- On average, smallholder farmers receiving fertilizer through the FSP had estimated incomes three times higher than the incomes of households who did not acquire fertilizer, and they had almost three times more land cropped per farm. The large percentage of farmers buying fertilizer and the relatively high incomes of those receiving FSP fertilizer suggest that most of the FSP recipients could have purchased fertilizer from private traders, like the larger group of farmers who actually did. Thus, it appears likely that the FSP program crowded out fertilizer sales by the private sector. A commercial fertilizer market is working, and many farmers have the means to purchase fertilizer.
- Farmers who reported buying fertilizer from dealers used less fertilizer than Farmers who received fertilizer through FSP, but they achieved comparable yields. This suggests that farmers who received fertilizer through the FSP used it less efficiently than farmers who purchased fertilizer.
- In round figures, the FSP distributed 50,000 metric tons of fertilizer during the 2002/03 cropping season. Each kilogram of fertilizer generated an average gain in maize yields of 1.3 kilogram, so the FSP as a whole resulted in an additional 65,000 metric tons of maize production.

(Continued)

- Valuation of fertilizer costs and the resulting maize gains suggest that spending on FSP fertilizer produced negative returns. In other words, the cost of the fertilizer distributed through the FSP greatly exceeded the value of the incremental maize produced.
- Because such a large share of the MACO budget is allocated to the FSP, other MACO activities—including agricultural extension and research—are severely underfunded and receive few operational resources.

Source: Jayne et al. 2006.

poorly developed. It would be very unusual to encounter this combination, because food markets are almost always present before input markets emerge.

Even in the very limited situations where the use of fertilizer might be used as a safety net, three additional issues need to be addressed:

- *Efficient use of resources.* Will public resources spent on fertilizer aid give the highest payoff relative to other alternatives (for example, providing oxen for overcoming a serious labor constraint or investment in irrigation for overcoming low yields)?
- *Effective targeting.* How can fertilizer subsidies be targeted effectively to reach the needy? What will prevent recipients of fertilizer subsidies from selling the fertilizer to obtain cash for use on other expenditures? Does it even matter if selling occurs?
- *Market-friendly.* How can fertilizer aid programs be designed so that they promote rather than undermine market development?

Two programs from Southern Africa—the Starter Pack/Targeted Inputs Program in Malawi and the Fertilizer Support Program in Zambia—illustrate the strengths and weaknesses of using fertilizer as an instrument for poverty alleviation and food security enhancement (boxes 7.3 and 7.4). Both programs succeeded in moving large amounts of fertilizer into the farming sector, and both programs stimulated sizable increases in maize production. At the same time, the fiscal and administrative costs of these programs were extremely high, and a large amount of subsidized fertilizer apparently went to wealthier farmers, including many who applied it to nonfood crops (Cromwell et al. 2001; Govereh et al. 2002; Levy and Barahona 2002).

Considering that fertilizer programs targeted at the poor have enjoyed a decidedly mixed record in Africa, what is the bottom line regarding fertilizer aid? Judging from experience, it is difficult to conclude that fertilizer is particularly effective as an instrument for pursuing welfare goals. On the contrary, it seems quite clear that the use of fertilizer policies to pursue welfare goals will be appropriate only in select circumstances, because fertilizer is generally not the most cost-effective instrument for alleviating poverty and reducing hunger. In the relatively uncommon cases where use of fertilizer as a safety net measure is justified, fertilizer should be distributed by using market-smart approaches that reduce poverty and hunger in the short run while vigorously stimulating the development of fertilizer markets over the longer run. Fertilizer promotion programs should be designed and implemented in ways that encourage increased use of fertilizer only in situations where fertilizer use is profitable, that stimulate rather than undermine the development of commercial input markets, and that contribute to the alleviation of structural constraints that are impeding the emergence of viable private sector–led fertilizer markets. Wherever possible, targeting mechanisms should be used to increase the likelihood that benefits will accrue to the poor, especially self-targeting methods that also reduce administrative costs and reduce opportunities for elite capture.

CHAPTER 8

Summary and Conclusions

This report has summarized key lessons learned from past efforts to promote increased fertilizer use in Africa, provided an overview of the current state of knowledge concerning technical aspects of fertilizer use in Africa, and presented good practice guidelines for promoting sustainable increases in fertilizer use.

The inherent lack of fertility of many African soils, which has been and continues to be exacerbated by widespread nutrient mining, has led to expansion of the agricultural frontier and the opening up of less favorable soils for cultivation. This is a scenario for disaster over the long run, given the difficulty of restoring tropical soils to productive capacity. In many tropical soils, the restoration of organic matter—a key component in soil fertility—is a very long-term proposal, and in lateritic soils such as those found throughout large parts of Africa, restoration may even be impossible. Without nutrient replenishment, many African farmers risk taking their soil resource base beyond a point of no return. Mainly for this reason, there is widespread agreement that the improvements in soil fertility needed to boost agricultural productivity growth, improve food security, and raise rural incomes will require substantial increases in fertilizer use, in combination with accelerated adoption of improved land husbandry practices. An additional implication is that soil fertility should be a priority not only for African policy makers but also for the development community more generally, because it would be difficult to justify continuing to invest in an agriculture that is exhausting its resource base.

There can be little doubt that fertilizer use must increase in Africa if the region is to meet its agricultural growth targets, poverty reduction goals, and environmental sustainability objectives. Policies and programs therefore are needed to encourage fertilizer use in ways that are technically efficient, economically rational, and market-friendly. At the same time, it is important to recognize that fertilizer is not a panacea for all of the problems that afflict African agriculture and that promoting fertilizer in isolation from other needed actions can have little lasting impact. Many fertilizer promotion schemes implemented in Africa have succeeded in temporarily increasing use of fertilizer, but only in ways that have encouraged inefficient use of fertilizer, imposed heavy administrative and fiscal burdens on governments, and undermined the development of viable private sector–led fertilizer markets. Such policies and programs are undesirable because they cannot be sustained over the longer term without large infusions of financial support that few African countries can afford.

Many initiatives have been launched to liberalize and privatize fertilizer markets in Africa, but relatively little progress has been made toward developing the type of enabling environment that is needed for a smooth and rapid transition from state-run to commercial input supply and output marketing systems. So what can be done? One important lesson that emerges from past efforts to promote increased fertilizer use in Africa is that there is a need for much clearer thinking about how fertilizer policy fits into a country's overall development strategy and goals. In recent years, expectations have increased regarding the role that fertilizer can play in the economic development process. Once viewed mainly as a productivity-enhancing input for agriculture, today fertilizer is seen by many policy makers and politicians as a tool that can be used to achieve a range of broad development goals, including stimulating rapid economic growth, alleviating poverty, and erecting safety nets to protect the rural poor in times of crisis. Some of these expectations are frankly unrealistic. Increased use of fertilizer can contribute to a range of objectives, including (in some cases) welfare objectives, but the size and the sustainability of the contribution that fertilizer can make will be limited as long as underlying structural problems in the economy remain unaddressed.

Many initiatives have been launched in Africa to remove fertilizer market distortions and harness the power of the private sector to procure fertilizer and deliver it to farmers, yet use of fertilizer continues to grow very slowly in most African countries. Why is this? Evidence reviewed in this report suggests that the low use of fertilizer in Africa can be explained by both demand-side and supply-side factors. Demand for fertilizer is often weak in Africa because incentives to use fertilizer are undermined by the low level and high variability of crop yields on the one hand and by the high level of fertilizer prices relative to crop prices on the other. The demand-depressing effects of unfavorable price incentives are aggravated by many other factors, including the general lack of market information about the availability and cost of fertilizer, the inability of many farmers to raise the resources needed to purchase fertilizer, and the lack of knowledge on the part of many farmers about how to use fertilizer efficiently. These constraints on the demand side are mirrored on the supply side by factors that reduce the timely availability of affordable fertilizer in the market. In many African countries, private investment in fertilizer distribution is discouraged by an unfavorable business climate characterized by poorly defined rules of the game, weak regulatory enforcement, a proliferation of taxes and fees, cumbersome bureaucratic procedures, a general lack of security, and the widespread incidence of corruption. In the absence of an active private fertilizer industry, fertilizer marketing is left mainly in the hands of inefficient public agencies and parastatals. More fundamentally—and regardless of whether it is being done by public agencies or private firms—fertilizer distribution is unprofitable in many parts of Africa because of the weak and dispersed nature of demand, the small market size, high transportation costs stemming from inadequate road and rail infrastructure, and the limited availability and high cost of financing.

What can be done to overcome weak demand for fertilizer on the one hand and inadequate supply on the other? In considering possible entry points for public interventions, it is important to adopt a long-term perspective. Past efforts to promote fertilizer in Africa all too often focused narrowly on stimulating immediate increases in fertilizer use with the help of fertilizer price subsidies—budgetary payments made by governments or development partners to reduce the cost of fertilizer at the farm level. This approach is very limited, however, because governments can do many things to promote fertilizer beyond artificially reducing the cost to farmers through direct price subsidies, and in fact other measures will often be more cost-effective and financially sustainable. Public interventions can be used to help farmers, but they can also be used to help fertilizer importers and manufacturers, fertilizer distributors at the wholesale and retail levels, financial services providers, and other key actors on the supply side. More fundamentally, public interventions can involve not only direct budgetary payments designed to influence fertilizer prices in the short run but also a wide range of other measures that improve the profitability of fertilizer over the medium to long run by directly or indirectly influencing market prices, costs incurred, or benefits received by consumers and producers of fertilizer. Many of these interventions have been discussed in this report.

Where does this leave fertilizer subsidies? Despite a history of disappointing results, fertilizer subsidies are now attracting renewed attention in Africa. Recently there has been considerable debate about the desirability of using fertilizer subsidies to achieve not only economic growth targets but also welfare goals. Although it is difficult to support the use of fertilizer subsidies on efficiency grounds, realistically it must be recognized that fertilizer subsidies are likely to be implemented in some African countries, if for no other reason than because of their political popularity.

Governments in Africa will not be able to tackle the problem of low fertilizer use merely by launching more fertilizer promotion schemes modeled on those that have been launched so many times in the past, particularly schemes that involve large-scale and indiscriminate use of subsidies on the price paid by farmers for fertilizer. Whenever direct price subsidies have been used to promote fertilizer, the results have almost always been disappointing: the cost of the subsidies has usually been high, and the benefits generated by the incremental fertilizer use have usually been modest. This does not mean that subsidies cannot at times play a useful role, however, provided they are used as part of a comprehensive and multifaceted approach that seeks to tackle the underlying root causes of low profitability of fertilizer. Although the long-term objective must be to support the emergence of viable private sector–led fertilizer markets, use of subsidies may be justifiable on a temporary basis to stimulate increased fertilizer use, provide income support to the poor, or both. This report has described a number of market-smart subsidies—measures that have been piloted with varying degrees of success in Africa to promote fertilizer. Examples include demonstration packs, vouchers, matching grants, and loan guarantees.

Subsidies may sometimes be justifiable in the short run as a second-best instrument for addressing the problem of low fertilizer use, but subsidies alone do not represent a long-term solution to the problem of missing fertilizer markets. Sustainable growth in fertilizer use in Africa is unlikely to happen unless resources can be shifted to activities that address the many underlying structural problems affecting incentives to supply fertilizer and to use fertilizer. These activities may include policy and institutional reforms, as well as public investment in infrastructure, knowledge generation and dissemination, capacity building, and improving the resource base on which African agriculture depends.

Policy reforms are needed to stimulate private investment in, and commercial financing of, the agricultural sector. Relevant options include trade policies that promote the free flow of goods, macroeconomic policies that facilitate access to foreign exchange, tax policies that do not place an undue tax burden on productive inputs, policies that promote competition by facilitating entry and exit of firms, and land tenure policies that increase farmers' access to credit and encourage increased agricultural investment.

Institutional reforms are needed to ensure smoothly functioning commercial exchanges at all levels of the value chain. Areas needing particular attention often include development and implementation of quality controls, enactment and enforcement of contract law, prevention of excessive consolidation of market power, and creation of farmers' cooperatives and professional organizations.

Investment in infrastructure is needed to reduce fertilizer costs, increase farmers' share of output prices, and improve the reliability of service (both timeliness of delivery and maintenance of quality of the product). Improvement of the entire range of transportation infrastructure is fundamental to these objectives, including improvement of rural roads, major highways, railways, and ports.

Strengthening in agricultural research and extension services is needed to improve their responsiveness to the needs of farmers and to allow them to adapt with greater agility to the commercial realities of the fertilizer sector. Some rethinking about how these services are organized and funded may be necessary, including consideration of public-private partnerships. Also some realigning of the criteria used to develop fertilizer recommendations may be needed to arrive at a cost-effective balance between farmers' need for location- and farm-specific recommendations and fertilizer suppliers' need to limit product variety to realize economies of scale.

Capacity building is needed to improve the knowledge and skills of farmers and commercial actors. Training needs typically differ by cropping system, level of market development, and infrastructure. Key needs include basic literacy and numeracy, business management training, and knowledge of fertilizer products. The problem must be addressed by improved public education systems, as well as through training programs that target farmers' and traders' needs.

Improvements in the agricultural resource base are needed to help improve the quality of soil and water resources so as to increase crop responses to fertilizer and reduce the risk of crop loss. The potential public-good nature of some of these improvements suggests that governments, possibly in partnership with the private sector, might need to be involved in irrigation and water control and in soil conservation and erosion control.

Readers of this report are to be wished good judgment in finding their way through the confusing maze of fertilizer policy making. It is hoped that the information distilled here will be helpful to those grappling with difficult fertilizer policy issues and that the companion *Africa Fertilizer Policy Toolkit* will be a useful resource for devising sound, practical interventions that will allow fertilizer to play the role that it must in the development of agriculture in Africa.

References

Alston, J. M., C. Chan-Kang, M. Marra, P. G. Pardey, and T. J. Wyatt. 2000. "A Meta-Analysis of Rates of Return to Agricultural R&D: Ex Pede Herculem?" Research Report 113, International Food Policy Research Institute (IFPRI), Washington, DC.

Anderson, J. R. 1989. "Reconsiderations on Risk Deductions in Public Project Appraisal." *Australian Journal of Agricultural Economics* 33 (2): 136–40.

Anderson, J. R., and J. B. Hardaker. 2003. "Risk Aversion in Economic Decision Making: Pragmatic Guides for Consistent Choice by Natural Resource Managers." In *Risk and Uncertainty in Environmental Economics*, ed. J. Wesseler, H.-P. Weikard, and R. Weaver, 171–88. Cheltenham, U.K.: Edward Elgar.

Anderson, J. R., R. W. Herdt, and G. M. Scobie. 1985. "The Contribution of International Agricultural Research to World Agriculture." *American Journal of Agricultural Economics* 67 (5): 1080–84.

———. 1988. *Science and Food: The CGIAR and its Partners.* Washington, DC: World Bank.

Angé, A. 1993. "Crunching the Numbers: A Realistic Biomass Budget Can't Overdraw on the World's Sources of Soil Nutrition." *Ceres* 25 (6).

Ariga, J., T. S. Jayne, and J. Nyoro. 2006. "Factors Driving the Growth in Fertilizer Consumption in Kenya, 1990–2005: Sustaining the Momentum in Kenya and Lessons for Broader Replicability in Sub-Saharan Africa." Working Paper

24/2006, Tegemeo Institute of Agricultural Policy and Development, Nairobi, Kenya.

Barbier, B. 1999. "Induced Innovation and Land Degradation: Results from a Bioeconomic Model of a Village in West Africa." *Agricultural Economics* 19 (1–2): 15–26.

Bationo, A., F. Lompo, and S. Koala. 1998. "Research on Nutrient Flows and Balances in West Africa: State-of-the-Art." *Agriculture, Ecosystems, and Environment* 71(1–3): 19–35.

Berthé, A. 2004. "Cost/Benefit Analysis of Ridge Tillage Adoption in Mali." PowerPoint presentation from Regional Scientific Workshop on Land Management for Carbon Sequestration, Bamako, Mali, February 26–27, organized by the USAID-funded SANREM CRSP.

Bingen, J., A. Serrano, and J. Howard. 2003. "Linking Farmers to Markets: Different Approaches to Human Capital Development." *Food Policy* 28: 405–19.

Binswanger, H., and D. A. Sillers. 1983. "Technological Priorities for Farming in Sub-Saharan Africa." *World Bank Research Observer* 3: 81–98.

Blackie, M. 2006. "Jump-Starting Maize Production in Malawi." Unpublished case study, prepared for Africa Fertilizer Strategy Assessment, World Bank, Washington, DC.

Breman, H. 1998. "Amélioration de la Fertilité de Sols en Afrique de l'Ouest: Contraintes et Perspectives." In *Soil Fertility Management in West African Land Use Systems*, ed. G. Renard, A. Neef, K. Becker, and M. v. Oppen. Weikersheim: Margraf Verlag.

Bumb, B. 1995. "Global Fertilizer Perspective, 1980–2000: The Challenges in Structural Transformation." Technical Bulletin T-42, IFDC, Muscle Shoals, AL.

Buresh, R., P. A. Sánchez, and F. Calhoun, eds. 1997. *Replenishing Soil Fertility in Africa.* Special Publication 51. Madison, WI: Soil Science Society of America (SSSA).

Byerlee, D., X. Diao, and C. Jackson. 2005. *Agriculture, Rural Development and Pro-poor Growth: Country Experiences in the Post-Reform Era.* Washington DC: World Bank.

Byerlee, D., and C. K. Eicher, eds. 1997. *Africa's Emerging Maize Revolution.* Boulder, CO: Lynne Rienner.

CIMMYT (Centro Internacional de Mejoramiento de Maíz y Trigo [International Maize and Wheat Improvement Center]). 1988. *From Agronomic Data to Farmer Recommendations: An Economics Training Manual.* Mexico City: CIMMYT.

Cleaver, K. M., and G. A. Schreiber. 1994. *Reversing the Spiral: The Population, Agriculture, and Environment Nexus in Sub-Saharan Africa.* Washington, DC: World Bank.

Coulter, J., A. Goodland, A. Tallontire, and R. Stringfellow. 1999. "Marrying Farmer Cooperation and Contract Farming for Service Provision in a Liberalising Sub-Saharan Africa." *Natural Resource Perspectives* (48, November). Overseas Development Institute (ODI), London. http://www. odi.org.uk/nrp/48.html.

Crawford, E. W., T. S. Jayne, and V. A. Kelly. 2006. "Alternative Approaches for Promoting Fertilizer Use in Africa." Agriculture and Rural Development Discussion Paper 22, World Bank, Washington, DC.

Crawford, E., V. Kelly, T. S. Jayne, and J. Howard. 2003. "Input Use and Market Development in Sub-Saharan Africa: An Overview." *Food Policy* 28: 277–92.

Croisson, P., and J. R. Anderson. 1999. "Land Degradation and Food Security: Economic Impacts of Watershed Degradation." In *International Watershed Management in the Global Ecosystem*, ed. R. Lal. Boca Raton, FL: CRC Press (for Soil and Water Conservation Society).

Cromwell, E., P. Kambewa, R. Mwanza, and R. Chirwa. 2001. "Impact Assessment Using Participatory Approaches: 'Starter Pack' and Sustainable Agriculture in Malawi." Network Paper 112, Agricultural Research & Extension Network, ODI, London.

Dalton, T. 1996. "Soil Degradation and Technical Change in Southern Mali." PhD diss., Department of Agricultural Economics, Purdue University, West Lafayette, IN.

Debra, K. 2002. "Agricultural Subsidies in Sub-Saharan Africa: A Reflection." PowerPoint presentation made at the Second Regional Meeting of Agro Inputs Trade Associations in West and Central Africa, Mercure Sarakawa Hotel, Lomé, Togo, December 5–6. IFDC Africa Division.

Dercon, S., and L. Christiaensen. 2005. "Consumption Risk, Technology Adoption And Poverty Traps: Evidence from Ethiopia." Draft paper, World Bank, Washington, DC.

Desai, G. M., and V. Gandhi. 1987. "Fertilizer Market Development and National Policy in China and India: A Comparative Perspective." Paper prepared for the IFA-FADINAP Southeast Asia and Pacific Regional Fertilizer Conference, July 22–25, Kuala Lumpur.

Donovan, G. 1996. "Agriculture and Economic Reform in Sub-Saharan Africa." AFTES Working Paper 18, World Bank, Washington, DC.

———. 2004. "Fertilizer Subsidies in Sub-Saharan Africa: A Policy Note." Draft paper, World Bank, Washington, DC.

Ellis, F. 1992. *Agricultural Policies in Developing Countries*. Cambridge: Cambridge University Press.

FAO (Food and Agriculture Organization). 1986. *African Agriculture: The Next 25 Years*. Annex V, Inputs Supply and Incentive Policies. Rome: FAO.

————. 2000. "The Challenges of Sustainable Forestry Development in Africa." Twenty-first FAO Regional Conference for Africa, FAO, Yaoundé, Cameroon.

————. 2002. *Fertilizer Use by Crop.* 5th ed. Rome: FAO (in collaboration with IFA, IFDC, IPI, and PPI).

————. 2003. *State of World Food and Agriculture.* Rome: FAO.

————. 2004. "Fertilizer Development in Support of the Comprehensive Africa Agriculture Development Programme (CAADP)." Proceedings of the 23rd Regional Conference for Africa, Johannesburg, South Africa, March 1–5, FAO, Rome.

————. 2005. "Increasing Fertilizer Use and Farmer Access in Sub-Saharan Africa: A Literature Review." Agricultural Management, Marketing, and Finance Service (AGSF), Agricultural Support Systems Division, FAO, Rome.

FAOSTAT. Statistical database. http://faostat.fao.org/.

Feder, G., and R. Slade. 1984. "The Acquisition of Information and the Adoption of New Technology." *American Journal of Agricultural Economics* 66 (3): 312–20.

Gisselquist, D., and C. Van der Meer. 2001. "Regulations for Seed and Fertilizer Markets: A Good Practice Guide for Policymakers." Rural Development Working Paper, World Bank, Washington, DC.

Gladwin, C. H., A. Randall, A. Schmitz, and G. E. Schuh. 2002. "Is Fertilizer a Public or Private Good in Africa? An Opinion Piece." *African Studies Quarterly* 6 (1, 2). http://www.africa.ufl.edu/asq/v6/v6i1a13.htm.

Govereh, J., and T. Jayne. 2003. "Cash Cropping and Food Crop Productivity: Synergies or Trade-offs?" *Agricultural Economics* 28 (1): 39–50.

Govereh, J., T. Jayne, J. Nijhoff, H. Haantuba, E. Ngulube, A. Belemu, J. Shawa, A. Banda, and B. Zulu. 2002. "Developments in Fertilizer Marketing in Zambia: Commercial Trading, Government Programs, and the Smallholder Farmer." Working Paper 4, Food Security Research Project, Lusaka, Zambia. http://www. aec.msu.edu/fs2/zambia/wp4zambia.pdf.

Gregory, D. I., and B. L. Bumb. 2006. "Factors Affecting Supply of Fertilizer in Sub-Saharan Africa." Agriculture and Rural Development, Discussion Paper 24, World Bank, Washington, DC.

Gruhn, P., F. Goletti, and M. Yudelman. 2000. "Integrated Nutrient Management, Soil Fertility, and Sustainable Agriculture: Current Issues and Future Challenges." Food, Agriculture, and the Environment, Discussion Paper 32, IFPRI, Washington, DC.

Gulati, A., and S. Narayanan. 2003. *The Subsidy Syndrome in Indian Agriculture.* New Delhi: Oxford University Press.

Heisey, P. W., and W. Mwangi. 1997. "Fertilizer Use and Maize Production in Sub-Saharan Africa." In *Africa's Emerging Maize Revolution,* ed. D. Byerlee and C. K. Eicher. Boulder, CO: Lynne Rienner.

Heisey, P. W., and G. Norton. Forthcoming. "Fertilizer and Other Farm Chemicals." In *Handbook of Agricultural Economics*, Vol. 3A, *Agricultural Development: Farmers, Farm Production, and Farm Markets*, ed. R. E. Evenson, P. Pingali, and T. P. Schultz. Amsterdam: Elsevier.

Henao, J., and C. Baanante. 2006. "Agricultural Production and Soil Nutrient Mining in Africa: Implications for Resource Conservation and Policy Development." IFDC, Muscle Shoals, AL.

Hess, U. 2003. "Innovative Financial Services for Rural India: Monsoon-Indexed Lending and Insurance for Smallholders." Agriculture and Rural Development Working Paper 9, World Bank, Washington, DC.

Hopper, D. 1993. "Indian Agriculture and Fertilizer: An Outsider's Observations." Keynote address to the Fertiliser Association of India (FAI) seminar on "Emerging Scenarios in Fertilizer and Agriculture: Global Dimensions," FAI, New Delhi.

Howard, J., J. Jeje, V. Kelly, and D. Boughton. 2000. "Comparing Yields and Profitability in MARD's High- and Low-Input Maize Programs: 1997/98 Survey Results and Analysis." Research Report 39, Ministry of Agriculture and Rural Development, Government of Mozambique, Maputo. http://www.aec.msu.edu/fs2/mozambique/flash/flash21e.pdf.

Howard, J., V. Kelly, J. Stepanek, E. Crawford, M. Demeke, and M. Maredia. 1999. "Green Revolution Technology Takes Root in Africa: The Promise and Challenge of the Ministry of Agriculture/SG2000 Experiment with Improved Cereals Technology in Ethiopia." International Development Working Paper 76, Department of Agricultural Economics, Michigan State University, East Lansing. http://www.aec.msu.edu/fs2/polsyn/number42.pdf.

Idachaba, F. S. 1974. "Policy Distortions, Subsidies, and African Rural Employment Creation: A Second-Best Approach." *Indian Journal of Agricultural Economics* 29 (2): 20–32.

IFDC (International Fertilizer Development Center). 2002. *Collaborative Research Programme for Soil Fertility Restoration and Management in Resource-Poor Areas of Sub-Saharan Africa.* Muscle Shoals, AL: IFDC.

———. 2003. "Input Subsidies and Agricultural Development: Issues and Options for Developing and Transitional Economies." Paper Series P-29, IFDC, Muscle Shoals, AL.

IFDC, IITA (International Institute for Tropical Agriculture), and WARDA (West Africa Rice Development Association). 2001. "Agricultural Input Markets in Nigeria: An Assessment and a Strategy for Development." Paper Series P-23, IFDC, Muscle Shoals, AL.

Jayne, T. S., J. Govereh, M. Wanzala, and M. Demeke. 2003. "Fertilizer Market Development: A Comparative Analysis of Ethiopia, Kenya, and Zambia." *Food Policy* 28 (4): 293–316.

Jayne, T. S., J. Govereh, Z. Xu, J. Ariga, and E. Mghenyi. 2006. "Factors Affecting Small Farmers' Use of Improved Maize Technologies: Evidence from Kenya and Zambia." Paper prepared for the organized symposium, "Seed/Fertilizer Technology, Cereal Productivity, and Pro-Poor Growth in Africa: Time for New Thinking?" 26th Conference of the International Association of Agricultural Economists (IAAE), Gold Coast, Queensland, Australia, August 12–18.

Jayne, T. S., and S. Jones. 1997. "Food Marketing and Pricing Policy in Eastern and Southern Africa: A Survey." *World Development* 25 (9): 1505–27.

Jayne, T. S., T. Yamano, and J. Nyoro. 2004. "Interlinked Credit and Farm Intensification: Evidence from Kenya." *Agricultural Economics* 31 (6): 209–18.

Kelly, V. A. 2006. "Factors Affecting Demand for Fertilizer in Sub-Saharan Africa." Agriculture and Rural Development Discussion Paper 23, World Bank, Washington, DC.

Kelly, V. A., and M. L. Morris. 2006. "Promoting Fertilizer to Increase Productivity in African Cereals Systems: What Role for Subsidies?" Paper prepared for the organized symposium, "Seed/Fertilizer Technology, Cereal Productivity, and Pro-Poor Growth in Africa: Time for New Thinking?" 26th Conference of the International Association of Agricultural Economists (IAAE), Gold Coast, Queensland, Australia, August 12–18.

Kelly, V., A. Adesina, and A. Gordon. 2003. "Expanding Access to Agricultural Inputs in Africa: A Review of Recent Market Development Experience." *Food Policy* 28 (4, August): 379–404.

Kessler, C. A., W. P. Spaan, W. F. van Driel, and L. Stroosnijder. 1995. "Choix et Modalités d'Exécution des Mesures de Conservation des Eaux et des Sols au Sahel: Une Comparaison de Cinq Projets de Développement." Tropical Resource Management Paper 8, Wageningen University, Wageningen, the Netherlands.

Kherallah, M., C. Delgado, E. Gabre-Madhin, N. Minot, and M. Johnson. 2002. *Reforming Agricultural Markets in Africa*. Baltimore: IFPRI and Johns Hopkins University Press.

Levy, S., ed. 2005. *Starter Packs: A Strategy to Fight Hunger in Developing Countries? Lessons from the Malawi Experience, 1998–2003*. Wallingford, Oxfordshire, U.K.: CABI Publishing.

Levy, S., and C. Barahona. 2002. *Findings of the Starter Pack and TIP M&E Programmes: Implications for Policy in 2002–03 and Beyond*. London: DFID.

MACO (Ministry of Agriculture and Cooperatives) (Zambia), ACF (Agricultural Consultative Forum), and FSRP (Food Security Research Project). 2002. "Developments in Fertilizer Marketing in Zambia: Commercial Trading, Government Programs, and the Smallholder Farmer." Working Paper 4, FSRP, Lusaka, Zambia. http://www.aec.msu.edu/fs2/zambia/wp4zambia.pdf.

Mann, C. 2003. "Smallholder Agriculture and Productivity Growth: Starter Pack in Malawi." Contribution to e-discussion on "Policies, Politics, Governance, and Accountability," part of Africa Fertilizer E-Forum sponsored by the World Bank on June 9, hosted by a group from Imperial College London, and organized as part of the Economic and Sector Work (ESW) under which this report is being produced.

Mazzucato, V., and D. Niemeijer. 2000. *Rethinking Soil and Water Conservation in a Changing Society: A Case Study in Eastern Burkina Faso*. Wageningen, the Netherlands: Wageningen University.

———. 2001. *Overestimating Land Degradation, Underestimating Farmers in the Sahel*. London: International Institute for Environment and Development (IIED).

McKean, M., and E. Ostrom. 1995. "Common Property Regimes in the Forest: Just a Relic from the Past?" *Unasylva* 180. http://www.fao.org/docrep/v3960e/v3960e03.htm#TopOfPage.

Meertens, B. 2005. "A Realistic View on Increasing Fertiliser Use in Sub-Saharan Africa." Paper presented on the Internet, December. www.meertensconsult.nl (select Debates).

Oygard, R., R. Garcia, A. Guttormsen, R. Kachule, A. Mwanaumo, I. Mwanawina, E. Sjaastad, and M. Wik. 2003. "The Maze of Maize: Improving Input and Output Market Access for Poor Smallholders in Southern Africa Region, the Experience of Zambia and Malawi." Report 26, Department of Economics and Resource Management, Agricultural University of Norway.

Pardey, P. G., and N. M. Beintema. 2001. "Slow Magic: Agricultural R&D a Century after Mendel." Food Policy Report, IFPRI, Washington, DC.

Pender, J., E. Nkonya, and M. Rosegrant. 2004. "Soil Fertility and Fertilizer Subsidies in Sub-Saharan Africa: Issues and Recommendations." PowerPoint presentation, IFPRI, Washington, DC.

Poulton, C., A. Dorward, and J. Kydd. 1998. "The Revival of Smallholder Cash Crops in Africa: Public and Private Roles in the Provision of Finance." *Journal of International Development* 10 (1): 85–103.

———. 2006. "Increasing Fertilizer Use in Africa: What Have We Learned?" Agriculture and Rural Development Discussion Paper 25. World Bank, Washington, DC.

Poulton, C., P. Gibbon, B. Hanyani-Mlambo, J. Kydd, W. Maro, M. Nylandsted Larsen, A. Osorio, D. Tschirley, and B. Zulu. 2004. "Competition and Coordination in Liberalized African Cotton Market Systems." *World Development* 32 (3): 519–36.

Robbins, P. 2000. *Review of Market Information Systems in Botswana, Ethiopia, Ghana, and Zimbabwe*. Wageningen, the Netherlands: Technical Center for Agricultural and Rural Cooperation.

Roumasset, J. A., M. W. Rosegrant, U. N. Chakravorty, and J. R. Anderson. 1989. "Fertilizer and Crop Yield Variability: A Review." In *Variability in Grain Yields: Implications for Agricultural Research and Policy in Developing Countries*, ed. J. R. Anderson and P. B. R. Hazell, 223–33. Baltimore: Johns Hopkins University Press (for IFPRI).

Sánchez, P., A. M. Izac, R. Buresh, K. Shepherd, M. Soule, U. Mokwunye, C. Palm, P. Woomer, and C. Nderitu. 1997. "Soil Fertility Replenishment in Africa as an Investment in Natural Resource Capital." In *Replenishing Soil Fertility in Africa*, ed. R. J. Buresh, P. A. Sánchez, and F. Calhoun. Madison, WI: SSSA.

Sansoni, S. 2002. "Silicon Mali." *Forbes Global* (February 4). Cited in World Bank (2006a), module 7, Agriculture Investment Note 7.5: "Getting Markets Right in the Post-Reform Era in Africa." http://www.forbes.com/global/2002/0204/042.html.

Scherr, S. 1999. "Soil Degradation: A Threat to Developing-Country Food Security by 2020?" Food, Agriculture, and the Environment Discussion Paper 27, IFPRI, Washington, DC.

Schultz, J. J., and D. H. Parish. 1989. "Fertilizer Production and Supply Constraints and Options in Sub-Saharan Africa." Paper Series P-10, IFDC, Muscle Shoals, AL.

Seward, P., and D. Okello. 1999. "SCODP's Mini-Pack Method: The First Step Towards Improved Food Security for Small Farmers in Western Kenya." Special Report 1, Sustainable Community-Oriented Development Programme (SCODP), Sega, Kenya.

Shalit, H., and H. Binswanger. 1984. "Fertilizer Subsidies: A Review of Policy Issues with Special Emphasis on Western Africa." Discussion Paper ARU 27, Research Unit, Agriculture and Rural Development Department, Operational Policy Staff, World Bank, Washington, DC.

Shepherd, A. 1997. "Market Information Services: Theory and Practice." Agricultural Services Bulletin 125, FAO, Rome.

Smaling, E. M. A., S. M. Nandwa, and B. H. Janssen. 1997. "Soil Fertility in Africa Is at Stake." In *Replenishing Soil Fertility in Africa*, ed. R. J. Buresh, P. A. Sánchez, and F. Calhoun. Madison, WI: SSSA.

Smith, J. 1994. "The Role of Technology in Agricultural Intensification: The Evolution of Maize Production in the Northern Guinea Savanna of Nigeria." *Economic Development and Cultural Change* 42 (3): 537–54.

Snapp, S. 1998. "Soil Nutrient Status of Smallholder Farms in Malawi." *Communications in Soil Science and Plant Analysis* 29 (17–18): 2571–88.

Stoorvogel, J. J., and E. M. A. Smaling. 1990. "Assessment of Soil Nutrient Depletion in Sub-Saharan Africa, 1983–2000." Report 28. Wageningen, the Netherlands: DLO Winand Staring Center for Integrated Land, Soil, and Water Research.

Stringfellow, R., J. Coulter, T. Lucey, C. McKone, and A. Hussain. 1997. "Improving the Access of Smallholders to Agricultural Services in Sub-Saharan Africa: Farmer Cooperation and the Role of the Donor Community." *Natural Resource Perspectives* (20, June). ODI, London.

Tomich, T. P., P. Kilby, and B. F. Johnston. 1995. *Transforming Agrarian Economies: Opportunities Seized, Opportunities Missed.* Ithaca, NY: Cornell University Press.

Townsend, R. F. 1999. "Agricultural Incentives in Sub-Saharan Africa: Policy Challenges." Technical Paper 444, World Bank, Washington, DC.

UN Millennium Project. 2005. "Halving Hunger: It Can Be Done." Report of the UN Millennium Project Task Force on Hunger, Earth Institute at Columbia University, New York. http://www.unmillenniumproject.org/reports/tf_hunger.htm.

UNEP (United Nations Environment Programme). 1997. *World Atlas of Desertification.* London: Arnold.

Van der Meer, K., and M. Noordam. 2004. "The Use of Grants to Address Market Failures: A Review of World Bank Rural Development Projects." Agriculture and Rural Development Discussion Paper 27, World Bank, Washington, DC.

van der Pol, F. 1992. *Soil Mining: An Unseen Contributor to Farm Income in Southern Mali.* Amsterdam: KIT (Koninklijk Instituut voor de Tropen [Royal Tropical Institute]).

Vierich, H. I. D., and W. A. Stoop. 1990. "Changes in West African Savanna Agriculture in Response to Growing Population and Continuing Low Rainfall." *Agriculture, Ecosystems & Environment* 31 (2): 115–32.

Weight, D., and V. Kelly. 1999. "Fertilizer Impacts on Soils and Crops of Sub-Saharan Africa." International Development Paper 21, Department of Agricultural Economics, Michigan State University, East Lansing.

World Bank. 2003. "Rural Financial Services: Implementing the Bank's Strategy to Reach the Rural Poor." Report 26030, Agriculture and Rural Development Department, Washington, DC.

———. 2005a. *Agricultural Growth for the Poor: An Agenda for Development.* Washington, DC: World Bank.

———. 2005b. *Meeting Development Challenges: Renewed Approaches to Rural Finance.* Washington, DC: World Bank.

———. 2005c. "Rural Finance Innovations: Topics and Case Studies." Report 32726-GLB, Agriculture and Rural Development Department, World Bank, Washington, DC.

———. 2006a. *Agriculture Investment Source Book.* Washington, DC: World Bank.

———. 2006b. *Agricultural Water for Poverty Reduction and Economic Growth in Sub-Saharan Africa.* Washington, DC: World Bank.

————. 2006c. *Ethiopia: Policies for Pro-Poor Agricultural Growth*. Washington, DC: World Bank.

————. 2006d. *Managing Food Price Risks and Instability in an Environment of Market Liberalization*. Washington, DC: World Bank.

Yanggen, D., V. Kelly, T. Reardon, A. Naseem, M. Lundberg, M. Maredia, J. Stepanek, and M. Wanzala. 1998. "Incentives for Fertilizer Use in Sub-Saharan Africa: A Review of Empirical Evidence on Fertilizer Response and Profitability." International Development Working Paper 70, Department of Agricultural Economics, Michigan State University, East Lansing.

Yesuf, M., A. Mekonnen, M. Kassie, and J. Pender. 2005. *Cost of Land Degradation in Ethiopia: A Critical Review of Past Studies*. Addis Ababa: Environmental Economics Policy Forum in Ethiopia and International Food Policy Research Institute.

Index

Boxes, figures, notes, and tables are indicated by b, f, n, and t, respectively.